KAE TEMPEST is a poet. They are also a writer, a lyricist, a performer and a recording artist. They have published plays, poems, a novel, a book-length non-fiction essay, released albums and toured extensively, selling out shows from Reykjavik to Rio de Janeiro. They received Mercury Music Prize nominations for both of the albums *Everybody Down* and *Let Them Eat Chaos*, and two Ivor Novello nominations for their song-writing on *The Book of Traps and Lessons*. They were named a Next Generation Poet in 2014, a once-in-a-decade accolade. They received the Ted Hughes Award for their long-form narrative poem *Brand New Ancients* and the Leone D'Argento at the Venice Teatro Biennale for their work as a playwright. Their books have been translated into eleven languages and published to critical acclaim around the world. They were born in London in 1985 where they still live. They hope to continue putting words together for a long time.

Kae Tempest

Paradise

A new version of Sophocles' *Philoctetes*

PICADOR

First published 2021 by Picador
an imprint of Pan Macmillan
The Smithson, 6 Briset Street, London EC1M 5NR
EU representative: Macmillan Publishers Ireland Ltd,
1st Floor, The Liffey Trust Centre, 117–126 Sheriff Street Upper,
Dublin 1, D01 YC43
Associated companies throughout the world
www.panmacmillan.com

ISBN 978-1-5290-4526-0

3 5 7 9 8 6 4 2

A CIP catalogue record for this book is available from the British Library.

Printed and bound by CPI Group (UK) Ltd, Croydon, CR0 4YY

Visit **www.picador.com** to read more about all our books
and to buy them. You will also find features, author interviews and
news of any author events, and you can sign up for e-newsletters
so that you're always first to hear about our new releases.

For my dad,
who always loved the old stories.

PARADISE

A new version of Sophocles' *Philoctetes*
by Kae Tempest

CAST IN ALPHABETICAL ORDER

The Soldiers

Odysseus **Anastasia Hille**
Neoptolemus **Gloria Obianyo**
Philoctetes **Lesley Sharp**

The Chorus

Magdalena **Claire-Louise Cordwell**
Aunty **ESKA**
Zuleika **Amie Francis**
Jelly **Sutra Gayle**
Shiloh **Jennifer Joseph**
Tishani **Sarah Lam**
Nam **Penny Layden**
Tayir **Kayla Meikle**
Yasmeen **Naomi Wirthner**

Director **Ian Rickson**
Set and Costume Designer **Rae Smith**
Lighting Designer **Mark Henderson**
Co-Composers **Stephen Warbeck** and **ESKA**
Movement **Coral Messam**
Sound Designer **Christopher Shutt**
Fight Director **Terry King**
Classical Adviser **Dr Helen Eastman**
Dramaturg **Stewart Pringle**
Associate Set Designer **Catherine Morgan**
Associate Costume Designer **Johanna Coe**
Staff Director **Danielle Baker-Charles**

Opening: Olivier Theatre, 11 August 2021

*A blank line of speech indicates that a character does not have the words.

Characters:

The Soldiers
    Philoctetes
    Odysseus
    Neoptolemus

The Chorus
    Aunty
    Jelly
    Nam
    Yasmeen
    Tishani
    Magdalena
    Shiloh
    Tayir
    Zuleika

The island; a bleak beach, rubbish-strewn, still in chaos from a huge wave that broke some years before. There are things where there shouldn't be: an old sink, corrugated iron, broken palms and rotting rubbish. On one side of the stage is the camp. On the other, the cave.

The cave is isolated, a gaping hole in the side of a difficult cliff, with a levelled plateau overlooking the beach.

The camp is a few flimsy tents surrounding a more permanent structure built from rubbish; there are mats, a carpet, a tarpaulin, a tin roof. The camp is well-kept and in order. Nine people live here. They are the CHORUS.

The cave is where PHILOCTETES lives. It is a mess; animal carcasses, petrol canisters, coconut shells and old food packaging lie where they have been thrown. There is a washing line strung up outside the entrance where blood-stained bandages hang drying.

It is just before dawn.

Some of the CHORUS are awake and sitting around the fire. The fire burns wood, plastic, all kinds of rubbish. Black smoke gets in their eyes, mouths, lungs.

Although the CHORUS have lived hard lives, they should not be played as 'downtrodden'. Some are worn out, their struggles more physically evident, others are glamorous. They all have dignity and, in general, a joyful presence.

AUNTY is the root from which the community has grown. She sits with a commanding presence, a part of but separate to the morning routine. She can see the audience. She can see through the barriers between worlds in a way that the others can't.

The CHORUS talk to each other with the ease of people that spend a great deal of time together. They don't need to hear the entirety of a line being said to intuit the meaning behind it. They do not necessarily wait for the ends of each other's lines. The actors playing these parts should trust their intuition about when to be tactile and playful with each other and when to take space.

TISHANI is tending the fire, MAGDALENA is brewing the tea, pouring it into cups and other makeshift vessels. JELLY is kneading a dough of rice flour and coconut water for bread.

YASMEEN	Good morning family.
TISHANI	Sleep all right?
YASMEEN	No.
TISHANI	Was it the sirens?
MAGDALENA	Bad dreams again?
YASMEEN	What sirens?
JELLY	Always complaining this one.
YASMEEN	I know you're not talking about me.
JELLY	First thing I hear from you on this beautiful morning is a complaint!
YASMEEN	What do you want me to do? Lie?
TAYIR	Someone must have tried to get over the prison wall.
MAGDALENA	It wasn't sirens.
SHILOH	I heard it.
MAGDALENA	It was the dogs howling. Because of the wind.
TISHANI	I didn't hear anything.
YASMEEN	I had nightmares again, that's all. Something bad was coming here.

[3]

SHILOH	That's the third time this week.
MAGDALENA	You need to drink water from the clay pot.
SHILOH	She's right. Draws the toxins out.
YASMEEN	What about you? How did you sleep?
ZULEIKA	Like a baby.
TISHANI	What happened to the grass?
JELLY	I thought it was helicopters again.
ZULEIKA	Remember last time? We better go and look.
TISHANI	What last time?
MAGDALENA	After the helicopters, I found all those coconuts.
ZULEIKA	I found them.
MAGDALENA	You weren't even / there
ZULEIKA	I was there.
MAGDALENA	I was on my own. I had to pick them up in my shirt and drag them / back down
ZULEIKA	No. I was with you. I remember.
SHILOH	It wasn't helicopters last night. It was the wind.

TISHANI	Must have been a big wind to blow the trees like that.
SHILOH	It was a big wind. It came from far out in the ocean.
JELLY	I rode in a helicopter once.
ZULEIKA	I *was* with you.
MAGDALENA	All right. You were with me then.
ZULEIKA	I knew it!
SHILOH	I slept fine, thanks for asking.
YASMEEN	Shiloh. How did you sleep?
SHILOH	No one ever asks me.
MAGDALENA	She just asked you.
SHILOH	Well, actually, I was up in the night. Something woke me.
TISHANI	What was it?
SHILOH	It was all of a sudden. You know that cold feeling you get when you wake up too fast? And now my shoulder's blocked again.
MAGDALENA	*(to TISHANI)* How's the neck?
TISHANI	It's OK.

MAGDALENA	So why are you sitting like that?
TISHANI	I'm not.
SHILOH	She's in pain.
TISHANI	No pain. It's just if I move here, like that, that's when it pulls.
YASMEEN	In a helicopter?
JELLY	In Montana. With the American. A private helicopter.
ZULEIKA	Aren't they all private?
JELLY	That man had so much money he didn't even know how much money he had.
ZULEIKA	Yeah, I'm like that.
MAGDALENA	Is it hurting now?
TISHANI	Only in the mornings. It'll be fine soon.
MAGDALENA	I made you a mixture for it.
NAM	*(waking)* You lot again.
YASMEEN	Morning.
NAM	Just once. Please God, just once.
YASMEEN	Just once what?

NAM   I just want to wake up and not see you lot.

JELLY   So go sleep somewhere else then.

TAYIR   *(sitting up, stretching)* Everyone's up.

MAGDALENA   Same as before but with turmeric root
               crushed in.

NAM   Does it work?

MAGDALENA   *(to TAYIR)* She asks me if my mixture
               works?

TAYIR   It worked for my back. I can move all the
               way round to there, look.

SHILOH   Not like that – you want to mix it with
               the aloe vera if you want it to / work

MAGDALENA   It works fine as it / is

SHILOH   And the green peppercorns. The green / ones

MAGDALENA   You've always got an opinion about my
               mixtures.

SHILOH   And what's wrong with that?

NAM   All that noise last night.

SHILOH   It was the wind.

NAM   It looks calm out there.

TAYIR   I dreamt of my husband again.

*JELLY, who is in her sixties but strong and young-spirited, makes
a vulgar gesture, full of mischief, one hand fucking the other,
caressing herself wildly. Gleeful with it. Some laugh at her.*

TISHANI   It's not funny. Don't encourage her.

TAYIR   Leave it out, we were dancing.

JELLY   Dancing!

*JELLY jumps up with her dough and begins to dance around them,
swinging her hips in and out and her boobs side to side and singing
the rhythm.*

JELLY   zicky zicky bah bah! zicky zicky bah bah!
                   When I was in the prison in Damascus,
                   I learnt the dancing from the Lebanese
                   women, like this.

She does it. Some laughter.

JELLY   And the men go.

*She dances the men's dance. Holding her arms out to the side and
rolling her shoulders. Cracking herself up.*

NAM   There any food yet?

*JELLY dances around to a sheet of metal that's resting on top of
an upturned petrol barrel where there are a few breads cooking,
she slaps another couple of discs down, making the rhythm all the
time – zicky zicky bah bah.*

MAGDALENA   You always make them too big, make them
             smaller.

JELLY   I like them big and thick.

Some laugh, some laugh at the futility of the laughter.

MAGDALENA   No they should be thinner.

JELLY   Your ones are too thin, they break. They're
             like biscuits.

YASMEEN   Now who's complaining?

SHILOH   I'm hungry. Thank you for cooking.

YASMEEN   Watch they don't dry out. How long have
             they been on?

TISHANI   I haven't slept deep enough to dream for
             years.

NAM   They look cooked to me.

She goes to take one but JELLY bats her away.

JELLY   Not yet. Sit down. Greedy. Get yours last.

*She lifts the breads from the pan and passes them out. They eat
slowly.*

The sky brightens.

JELLY   Sun's coming up.

ZULEIKA   Aunty! The sun's rising.

AUNTY   This island screams and screams all night.
                 Its head is fire, its chest is tight,
                 Its teeth are expired dynamite.
                 Its nails are blunt, its figure slight,
                 A shadow of its former might.

                 Big city once, this place. It was.
                 Did roaring trade. Us lot had jobs
                 And kids and kept our homes well stocked.
                 Then the war crossed over us,
                 We crossed ourselves. The gods were dead.
                 They cut the mains, the power surged
                 And everything was white and red.

                 Then the big wave broke
                 And sucked the land into the sea.

                 Then the marches started.
                 The partial-hearted starved, people grew
                     guarded,
                 Aircraft scarred the skyline.

                 The hardship of the times was like a car
                     crash we'd invited.
                 Staring at the carnage like it was something
                     on TV.
                 Wasn't my problem.
                 Till it happened to me.

                 Then everything was flags.
                 They shouted till they puked.
                 A thousand deadbeat dreary boys in
                     uniforms and boots.

Men left here in cars and trucks and boats
  they built from scrap.
The kids were sent to forge ahead,
No passport, food, or map.
I like to think that some day, one or two
  might make it back.

If you could, you paid in gold,
Crumpled notes and sweat.
Smuggled out at dawn,
With nothing left but debt.

Any vessel, bound elsewhere.
Somewhere you could breathe the air.

We've tried to leave so many times.
Just can't get the visas.
We've all seen cells and hospitals.
None of it's been easy.

True enough, you live as long as us,
You learn some tricks.
I hid out in the desert for a bit till I got sick.

These days, it's just a vacant place –
An island rich with human poor.
The world dumps all its plastic waste
And takes a couple hundred more.
Fair exchange, I suppose,
We're all just rubbish on the shore.

Nasty times we've landed in.
Landfill life, the whole damn thing's a joke.
Signals in the smoke
Say *you can't fix it till it's broke.*

Most weeks you get a drama here.
I've seen my share. Don't ask.

It's taught me good from year to year.
At best the worst has passed.

Today a drama's coming on.
It's in my ankles, look?
All swollen up. See? Something's wrong.
Last night each red branch shook,
But not one green branch moved.

I see it.

I can see them coming.

Two strangers break off from the pack.
The prophecy, the distant drumming,
Tells them to attack.

Days turn inwards, endless boredom.
Out there, only sea.
The troops cheered as they left the camp,
Said it was meant to be.

Their thin black ship cuts tides in half.
The young one's sick for shore.
The elder's been kept far too long from home
    in blood and war.

Two soldiers coming closer for that soldier in
    the cave.
I see the water rising,
Its mouth an open grave.

The waves are tall but fall away.
The rain relentless buckshot spray.
The wind is thick. Dark purple grey.
Nature gives her warnings but the men
    don't watch the play.
They watch the pictures in their minds
    instead, as is their way.

They come from the unending war,
They're heading for our beach.
They want the wounded one.
They'll trick him with their speech.

They'll be here soon enough,
I see they're scheming on his bow.
That's good news for us,
We get to sit and watch the show.

*ODYSSEUS and NEOPTOLEMUS dock their boat and walk up
the beach.*

ODYSSEUS   Nothing beats the stench of sewage after
                 a month at sea.

He slaps his arms, neck, legs after a biting insect.

ODYSSEUS   Charming place.

*They walk past the CHORUS who stare at them. NEOPTOLEMUS
offers a nod.*

ODYSSEUS   I wouldn't. They'll only take it for weakness.

*The two men come to a stop. The CHORUS ignore them. Getting on
with things.*

ODYSSEUS   This is your first time out.

NEOPTOLEMUS   Yes sir.

ODYSSEUS   Do you feel up to it?

NEOPTOLEMUS   Never been readier.

ODYSSEUS   Good. That's the attitude.

NEOPTOLEMUS   My whole life I've been waiting for this
                moment sir.

ODYSSEUS   Well, it has arrived. Bask in it.

NEOPTOLEMUS

ODYSSEUS   So let's go over it one more time. Why are
                we here?

NEOPTOLEMUS   The prophecy. There is a man here. We need
                to capture him.

ODYSSEUS   Is he our enemy?

NEOPTOLEMUS   Potentially.

ODYSSEUS   Is he our friend?

NEOPTOLEMUS   We need him.

ODYSSEUS   Are we here to kill him?

NEOPTOLEMUS   No. We need him alive. Able to fight.
                With his weapon.

[14]

ODYSSEUS   Why is he here?

NEOPTOLEMUS   You left him here.

ODYSSEUS   Very good.

NEOPTOLEMUS   Thank you sir.

ODYSSEUS   When they gave me your name for this,
                I thought to myself, and I don't mind
                telling you, I thought, oh fuck! You know?
                Fuck me!

                And let's be honest, you're not much on
                paper, are you?

NEOPTOLEMUS   I wouldn't know sir, I've not seen my files.

ODYSSEUS   Well, take it from me, there's not much
                to them. But there will be! After this.

NEOPTOLEMUS   I just need my chance. That's all.

ODYSSEUS   I know that me and you didn't really get
                off to the best start, but life in the army is
                about earning your stripes. You're not born
                entitled to my respect. You have to earn it,
                like everybody else. No matter who your
                father is.

NEOPTOLEMUS   Just let me get out there. I'll make them pay.
                You wait and see. I'll / make them

ODYSSEUS   Anyway, someone must have seen something
                in you, because here we are! Aren't we?

[15]

NEOPTOLEMUS Yes sir.

ODYSSEUS points to the cave.

ODYSSEUS That's where he lives. Like an animal.

They survey it.

ODYSSEUS Get up there and have a look around. If he sees you, he'll kill you. Is that clear?

NEOPTOLEMUS You want me to go up there?

ODYSSEUS

NEOPTOLEMUS Up there and find him and bring him back down?

ODYSSEUS Just go and have a look and report back to me.

NEOPTOLEMUS Yes sir. Reconnaissance. Got it.

ODYSSEUS Don't be seen.

NEOPTOLEMUS makes his way to the cave. ODYSSEUS takes a flask from his hip. Swigs deeply, privately. Troubled by being back on this island again.

ZULEIKA I wouldn't climb it that way.

SHILOH It's just piles of muck and thorny scrub.

NAM That drags the land from beach to cliff.

JELLY	Plants like knives, and rocks like sand.
ZULEIKA	And snarling vines that fool your hand.
TAYIR	Broken arrows, poisoned tips.
JELLY	Best be careful. Dead if he slips.
TISHANI	Stop looking at them.

NEOPTOLEMUS returns.

ODYSSEUS	Well?
NEOPTOLEMUS	Not much to it. Blood-soaked rags on every hook. Old cardboard to sleep on.
ODYSSEUS	Him?
NEOPTOLEMUS	Not there. But the firepit's warm.
ODYSSEUS	He can't go far on that leg.
NEOPTOLEMUS	It stinks.
ODYSSEUS	I'm sure it does.
NEOPTOLEMUS	I've never smelt anything / like it
ODYSSEUS	You know, before all this − he had a vineyard and bred horses.
NEOPTOLEMUS	He must hate you.
ODYSSEUS	What?

NEOPTOLEMUS   What?

ODYSSEUS   What did you just say?

NEOPTOLEMUS   Nothing. I was just saying that if you left
              him here. And before you left him, he had
              a lovely life and now he lives up there . . .

NEOPTOLEMUS catches the look ODYSSEUS throws at him.

NEOPTOLEMUS   Nothing.

ODYSSEUS   Nothing what?

NEOPTOLEMUS   Nothing sir.

Beat.

ODYSSEUS   Do you know how long I've been fighting
              this war?

NEOPTOLEMUS   Twelve years sir?

ODYSSEUS   And in all that time, how many operations
              do you think I've been on?

NEOPTOLEMUS   Countless?

ODYSSEUS   Too many to count. And yet, *this* is the
              most significant operation of them all.
              Do you see that?

NEOPTOLEMUS   Absolutely.

ODYSSEUS   What do you see?

NEOPTOLEMUS   I see victory. We're destined for it.

ODYSSEUS   I don't know how much longer we can
              hold out.

NEOPTOLEMUS

ODYSSEUS   There's been so much death these last two
              years. Unspeakable injuries. It's got to the
              troops. There's been desertion at the front.
              We're in bad shape. It's hard to keep fighting
              when it feels like the gods are for the other
              team.

NEOPTOLEMUS   I thought we were winning?

ODYSSEUS   But! If we get to the front with him and
              that weapon of his we're the chosen ones
              again! Do you see? The troops need a sign,
              something they can get behind. Philoctetes
              could take thirty men with *one* shot. You
              should have seen him on the battlefield,
              he was unbelievable. He could be in five
              places at once, and he knew how to keep
              his team with him, full of encouragement,
              and dropping back to push the stragglers
              on, then up front again, like he'd never left.
              He was a beast, a machine! Just his name
              can make a soldier push for that last bit of
              strength they didn't think they had left.
              Imagine his *presence*.

*ODYSSEUS squares up to NEOPTOLEMUS. Terrifying, sudden
aggression.*

ODYSSEUS   Do you understand me?

NEOPTOLEMUS Yes sir, I understand. Crystal.

ODYSSEUS   What are we here to do?

NEOPTOLEMUS Get Philoctetes and his weapon and take
                            him to the front.

ODYSSEUS   What happens if we fail?

NEOPTOLEMUS We can't fail.

ODYSSEUS   Good lad.

*ODYSSEUS drinks from his flask again, hands it to
NEOPTOLEMUS, who also drinks.*

TISHANI   Oh God help me.

MAGDALENA   What?

TISHANI   Tedious.

SHILOH   Stop listening to it then.

TISHANI   I can't exactly stop can I, they're *there*.

NAM   Like they own the place.

JELLY   Move then.

TISHANI   Why should *I* move?

SHILOH   Why can't they move?

TAYIR	I want to move.
ODYSSEUS	We can't take him by force, and I can't risk an ambush. I need you *both* alive. If he sees me or gets a hint of my being anywhere near this, we're done for. It's over.
NEOPTOLEMUS	Yes, I understand sir.
ODYSSEUS	The only way this is going to work is by you taking a deep breath and going in alone.
NEOPTOLEMUS	Me? Alone?
ODYSSEUS	Here it is! Your chance to step out from under your father's shadow and really prove yourself.
NEOPTOLEMUS	
ODYSSEUS	Don't look like that. I could think of a thousand soldiers who'd kill themselves for this opportunity.
NEOPTOLEMUS	What if I can't do it?
ODYSSEUS	I know you can do it.
NEOPTOLEMUS	*(with rising aggression)* I am ready.
ODYSSEUS	*(matching the aggression)* What are you ready for?
NEOPTOLEMUS	*(pushing it further)* I am ready to do this for my country.

SHILOH   All right, keep your bloody hair on.

ZULEIKA   All went a bit Rambo for a minute there
                didn't it.

TISHANI   Don't talk to them. Don't even look at
                them.

ODYSSEUS   Now, this is what we're going to do: first
                thing is, you find him and you engage him
                in conversation. When he asks you who
                you are, tell him the truth – I am the son
                of Achilles, give him all the pomp and
                ceremony, he'll love that.

NEOPTOLEMUS Do I have to mention him?

ODYSSEUS   Yes. You do. Tell him you're on your way
                home, that you're AWOL from the army.
                That you left the battleground in a rage.
                Swaying like a taunted bull. Tell him how
                they begged you to enlist, how they told
                you that now your dad was dead, *you* were
                the *only one* who could win the war, and
                so you joined up – but when you asked for
                your father's armour, yours by right, by
                holy right, they kept it from you.

He opens his jacket, revealing the armour.

                Beautiful, isn't it? Swirls of dark metal,
                blood-washed to bronze. Your succession
                to man. The war orphan's glory; to become
                what was taken from him.

But as you watched, the generals hung
your father's shining armour on Odysseus'
shoulders.

You remember, don't you?

Odysseus! That slimy careerist, that snake,
that dirty no good swine of a general, etc.
etc., that perverted fiend, hell-bent on glory,
took what was yours and left you and your
father's memory desecrated.

Didn't he?

ODYSSEUS spits on the floor by NEOPTOLEMUS' feet.

All coming back now, is it?

NEOPTOLEMUS nods.

Good.

And so, you absconded and are sailing home.
And you stopped here by chance. By *chance.*
On your way.

You understand the story?

NEOPTOLEMUS The more I convince him of how much I hate
you, the better for the plan?

ODYSSEUS That's right. Very good. Shouldn't be too
hard, should it?

NEOPTOLEMUS No sir.

Beat.

ODYSSEUS   What is it?

NEOPTOLEMUS

ODYSSEUS   I asked you a question.

NEOPTOLEMUS It's not right.

ODYSSEUS   What's not right?

NEOPTOLEMUS Deceiving him. Making him think I'm here by accident.

ODYSSEUS

NEOPTOLEMUS

ODYSSEUS   You tell one lie to one man, you save the entire nation.

NEOPTOLEMUS I don't like lying to people. I'm no good at it.

ODYSSEUS   There is no other way of doing this.

NEOPTOLEMUS It feels. Underhand.

ODYSSEUS   Once we've got him out there, and the battle's ours, everyone will thank you for it. Including him.

NEOPTOLEMUS But if he comes with me because he trusts me, then I break his trust, what does it make me?

[24]

ODYSSEUS   It will make you a hero.

NEOPTOLEMUS   A hero. But you're either honest, or you're
                not. What's my word worth if I can break it
                any time I like?

ODYSSEUS   These are your orders.

NEOPTOLEMUS   Yes sir.

ODYSSEUS   And you have sworn to what?

NEOPTOLEMUS   Obey.

ODYSSEUS   That's right. And what else?

NEOPTOLEMUS   To preserve and protect my country, and
                defend against all enemies.

ODYSSEUS   That is exactly what we're doing here.
                Protecting. Defending.

NEOPTOLEMUS   Yes sir. But /

ODYSSEUS   Right now, *right now*, some poor kid's just
                had his belly ripped open, his mate's had her
                leg blown off, his other mate's just been shot
                in the throat and he's watching them scream
                their last words out of their new mouth.
                That's happening *right now* and it's going to
                keep on happening until we complete this
                mission.

NEOPTOLEMUS   Yes sir.

ODYSSEUS   Everything you love; gone. Your people,
                 speaking the enemy's language. Washing the
                 enemy's floors. Everything your dad gave
                 his life to fight for, it will all have been for
                 nothing. Do you understand?

NEOPTOLEMUS   What if he knows it's a trap sir?

ODYSSEUS   He won't. You just need get him in the boat.

NEOPTOLEMUS   Yes sir.

ODYSSEUS   Remember, this man is not our friend, he is
                 our weapon. OK? So, we treat him like we
                 treat any other weapon. Clean him, store
                 him, transport him safely, take him into
                 battle. And that's it.

                 And watch out for those lot, even their
                 diseases have diseases.

NEOPTOLEMUS   What, you're going?

JELLY   Already?

TAYIR   So soon?

ODYSSEUS   Yes I'm going. I'll be waiting on the ship.

SHILOH   He's scared.

NAM   Doesn't want to face him again after all
                 these years.

TISHANI   Stop it.

ZULEIKA   He's sending you in as bait.

NEOPTOLEMUS How will I find him?

NAM   You can't miss him.

ODYSSEUS   He lives in that cave.

NAM   That one, over there. With all the bones
                 outside.

ODYSSEUS   All you've got to do is persuade him you're
                 on the same side and offer him a ride home.

JELLY   *All* you've got to do, you know.

ODYSSEUS disarms him.

NEOPTOLEMUS

ODYSSEUS   Trust me, you'll be safer without it.
                 And your knife.

ODYSSEUS reaches inside his jacket and takes his knife.

NEOPTOLEMUS

JELLY   He took his knife!

ZULEIKA   What did I say? Bait.

YASMEEN   No he's right to take it.

JELLY   Why?

YASMEEN	Because Philoctetes will find it on him, and then he'll kill him for it.
TAYIR	But how can he leave him out here with nothing?
NEOPTOLEMUS	Are you really leaving me out here with nothing?
ODYSSEUS	Your dad would be proud if he could see you now, standing up for us like this.
NEOPTOLEMUS	He would.
ODYSSEUS	You're about to surprise yourself.
NEOPTOLEMUS	This will be the making of me.
ODYSSEUS	It will.
NEOPTOLEMUS	I'd do anything for my country.
ODYSSEUS	Do this.

ODYSSEUS leaves.

MAGDALENA	Why don't you come and sit down?
TISHANI	Don't.
JELLY	We're not gonna bite.
ZULEIKA	Well, she might.
JELLY	No chance, I've not got my teeth in.

MAGDALENA   Come on, come and sit down over here.

TISHANI   You shouldn't be doing this.

ZULEIKA   We're just having a bit of fun.

TISHANI   Something bad will happen.

MAGDALENA   This one's different. He's open.

TISHANI   They're killers.

MAGDALENA   It's OK.

TISHANI   Don't touch me.

TISHANI makes space between herself and the group.

TAYIR   He can help us.

NAM   How?

TAYIR   *(to NEOPTOLEMUS)* We know who you're
                   looking for.

JELLY   We can help you find him.

*NEOPTOLEMUS tries to ignore them, falls to studying tracks left
by something heavy walking up the beach. He bends over them.*

ZULEIKA   That's pig tracks! Your man went that way.

NEOPTOLEMUS looks over.

ZULEIKA   Over there! I can show you. but you're better
                   off waiting here. He'll be back any minute.

NEOPTOLEMUS   I don't know who you're talking about.

MAGDALENA   Your man from the cave. He went that way.

NEOPTOLEMUS   Which way?

NAM   Leave him be, poor boy.

TISHANI burns some herbs.

TISHANI   Forgive us.

JELLY   He's all right.

ZULEIKA   Come and sit down!

NEOPTOLEMUS   No, thank you.

JELLY   Why not?

NEOPTOLEMUS   I can't. I'm under orders.

NEOPTOLEMUS edges closer to them, in spite of himself.

TAYIR   He hunts at night, it's morning now.
He'll be back soon.

NEOPTOLEMUS   Back at the cave?

TAYIR   Yep.

NEOPTOLEMUS   Which direction do you think he'll be
coming from?

NAM   Tell us your name first?

NEOPTOLEMUS   Neoptolemus.

A couple of 'oooohs' at his fancy name.

TAYIR   What you stopped here for?

NEOPTOLEMUS   Nothing.

MAGDALENA   Nothing?

NEOPTOLEMUS   I come in peace.

NAM   *(to TISHANI)* See? He comes in peace!

YASMEEN   Dressed like that?

NEOPTOLEMUS   There's a big war, over the sea. I'm a soldier.

NAM   Seas full of bodies now son, you won't get far in your boat.

ZULEIKA   Where is there a war?

YASMEEN   Always a war somewhere.

MAGDALENA   Not here there's not. War's over.

JELLY   What you got in your pockets Neoptolemus?

NEOPTOLEMUS   Nothing.

TAYIR   What, no papers?

NEOPTOLEMUS   No, just my hands.

TAYIR	Let's have a look then.
JELLY	Lovely hands he's got.
NAM	I could do with a pair of hands like that.
JELLY	I wouldn't mind a few of those fingers.
ZULEIKA	Ignore them, they're harmless. Silly old bunch.
NEOPTOLEMUS	If you could tell me, I'd be grateful – where will I find him?
ZULEIKA	I told you. He went that way. But he'll be back before the sun reaches the low branches.
NEOPTOLEMUS	Thank you.
ZULEIKA	You're welcome.
MAGDALENA	Lovely manners he's got.
NAM	What does he want? Who's he come for again?
ZULEIKA	You know who!
MAGDALENA	Philoctetes.
JELLY	The sufferer!
TAYIR	Everybody suffers, he dwells. That's his problem. The / dweller
NAM	Oh *him*! What does he want him for? I won't go near / him

[32]

JELLY	He won't go near you more / like!
MAGDALENA	I think he's scared of / us
TAYIR	Wonder why?
SHILOH	We don't know that much about him, he never talks to / us
NAM	Not even a smile.
MAGDALENA	I feel sorry for / him
JELLY	Sorry for *him*, she says.
MAGDALENA	I do. Poor love. He's like a / child
SHILOH	Time he learnt. You'd think, by *now*. Ten years if it's / a day
NAM	Do you have any chocolate?
NEOPTOLEMUS	No, I'm sorry I don't.
NAM	Whisky?
NEOPTOLEMUS	No.
NAM	What about a couple of coins then? Spare a few quid for an old dear?

He roots around for change, hands some coins to NAM who places them in a circle around the fire. The ritual is absorbing.

NEOPTOLEMUS How long have you been here?

TAYIR   I was born here.

NEOPTOLEMUS   Here?

TAYIR   Not in the camp. We lived in the North.
                By the port.

SHILOH   She was born the wrong way round.

TAYIR   That's right. Feet first. Ready to run.

JELLY   Sensible.

NAM   In the old hospital, which had very big
                windows.

TAYIR   Mum was on shift when her waters broke.

ZULEIKA   She came early.

MAGDALENA   Only time in her life she hasn't been late.

JELLY   They had to turn her around.

TAYIR   I was early yes. And they turned me around.
                Ever since / then

JELLY   She never knows which way she's going.

NEOPTOLEMUS   *(indicating AUNTY)* And her?

AUNTY smiles at him. Interested. Like he's a harmless little animal that has wandered into the camp. She makes a sign in the air. He is warmed by her attention. They share an energetic exchange.

[34]

NEOPTOLEMUS	And the rest of you – were you born here too?
SHILOH	I've always been here.
NAM	It was a different time. Before the men left.
YASMEEN	Her father named her.
SHILOH	Lifted me in his arms and whispered my name into my ear.
NEOPTOLEMUS	Does your name have a meaning?
SHILOH	Of course.
NEOPTOLEMUS	What does it mean?
JELLY	Her name means peace.
NEOPTOLEMUS	Your father named you peace?
SHILOH	He did.
NEOPTOLEMUS	What did he do?
SHILOH	He was a soldier.
NEOPTOLEMUS	Mine too.
SHILOH	He's dead now.
NEOPTOLEMUS	Mine too.
SHILOH	Does your name have a meaning?

NEOPTOLEMUS   It does.

YASMEEN   What does it mean?

NEOPTOLEMUS   It means war.

JELLY   That's a heavy name to hang around a child.

NEOPTOLEMUS   It's a long story.

SHILOH   Well, we're very busy people.

NAM   Tell us.

NEOPTOLEMUS   I'm not supposed to be talking to you.

NAM   We're not supposed to be talking to you
              either.

YASMEEN   So that makes us even.

MAGDALENA   I'm drinking. Who's drinking?

SHILOH   Me. I will.

*MAGDALENA pours out cups of homebrew. Relights the
stubbed-out joint she has tucked down her bra. Offers it to
NEOPTOLEMUS.*

TAYIR   Where were you born?

NEOPTOLEMUS   At home.

TAYIR   What's home like?

NEOPTOLEMUS   Home is a big house with high walls,
               built on top of a hill that looks over a city.

JELLY   Go on.

NEOPTOLEMUS   The house is made of yellow stone. There are
               lots and lots of empty rooms that have to be
               swept and dusted every day. It's just me and
               Mum in that big old house. There are three
               cooks, who feed us like we have no hands.

NAM   That must be very hard for you both.

NEOPTOLEMUS   Sometimes when I'm there, I feel like I'm
               suffocating. It's not like this. Out here. All
               this air to breathe. I didn't know that people
               lived outside like this.

MAGDALENA   Oh it's all the rage in this part of the world.

SHILOH   But why did he call you like that?

NEOPTOLEMUS   Because the only thing he wanted for me is
               that I would grow up to be a fighter like him.

NAM   And here you are.

TAYIR   We knew you were coming to get him.

NEOPTOLEMUS   I don't know what you're talking about.

ZULEIKA   We have a prophet too. Just like you.

JELLY   Except we don't keep ours in chains in
               a dark room.

[37]

NAM   Don't worry, we won't tell him.

NEOPTOLEMUS I've come to take him home. That's all.

SHILOH   You sure about that?

NEOPTOLEMUS He should never have been so long on his own.

*PHILOCTETES enters silently, dragging his leg, he sees
NEOPTOLEMUS and freezes. In one motion, he sets an arrow in
his bow and aims. Unseen.*

TAYIR   Can I come?

NEOPTOLEMUS What?

TAYIR   I would like to come with you.

NEOPTOLEMUS Where?

TAYIR   I'm serious. Can you take me with you when
               you leave here?

NEOPTOLEMUS I don't know, I wouldn't even know where
               to / begin

SHILOH   He's a prince! A rescuer, at last!

NAM   Can't you take us all Prince?

SHILOH   Where's your glass slipper?

*SHILOH picks up an old banana peel from the floor and drapes it
over her foot. ZULEIKA snatches it from her.*

ZULEIKA   A glass slipper!! Yes, let me try. It fits me!
                     It fits!!! *I* want to go to the ball.

TAYIR   *(to NEOPTOLEMUS)* I want a life.

JELLY   She wants the brand-new phone with the
                     synched-up laptop, the box-fresh kicks and
                     the SUV.

*PHILOCTETES steps further into the scene until he is directly
behind NEOPTOLEMUS, the arrow drawn and levelled at the
back of his head.*

TAYIR   And what's wrong with that? What's *wrong*
                     with wanting that? Rest of the world has
                     that. Rest of the world has *underground
                     trains*. My husband told me all about it. I
                     want to go for coffee in that place, there's a
                     place with a green mermaid sign and it has
                     glass walls, the whole front wall is made of
                     glass. I could get a job there. I could get a
                     washing machine, *I* could get a flat-screen
                     TV. I could get food cooked for me and
                     delivered to my *door*. My husband sent me
                     a letter all about it / before he

SHILOH   It's all right babe, it's OK.

NEOPTOLEMUS   Look I'll see what I can do, but I really can't
                     promise / any

NEOPTOLEMUS feels the point of the arrow.

PHILOCTETES   Stand up. Slowly.

NEOPTOLEMUS stands slowly.

PHILOCTETES   Turn.

NEOPTOLEMUS turns to stare the arrow down.

PHILOCTETES   Who are you?

NEOPTOLEMUS   A soldier, from the /

PHILOCTETES   What are you doing here?

NEOPTOLEMUS   I landed by mistake.

PHILOCTETES   No you didn't. Who are you?

NEOPTOLEMUS   A soldier. I'm on my way home.

PHILOCTETES   Why have you come here?

NEOPTOLEMUS   I don't know. I just docked up.

PHILOCTETES   You don't know?

NEOPTOLEMUS   By accident. My ship.

ZULEIKA   People don't come here. People try and leave here.

NEOPTOLEMUS   I'm on the run. I'm trying to get home. I've been at sea for months. I got lost in a bad storm. I ran out of food. I saw the buildings.

PHILOCTETES   Where's the boat?

NEOPTOLEMUS   Around that headland, there.

PHILOCTETES   What do you mean you're on the run?

NEOPTOLEMUS   I was betrayed.

PHILOCTETES   Are you armed?

NEOPTOLEMUS   No sir.

PHILOCTETES   Why not?

NEOPTOLEMUS   I /

PHILOCTETES   Lift your jacket slowly, show me the belt of your trousers.

He does.

PHILOCTETES   Turn around slowly, all the way.

He does.

PHILOCTETES   Lift your trouser legs, one at a time, show me your ankles.

He does.

PHILOCTETES   Betrayed by who?

NEOPTOLEMUS   My generals. At the front. I'm just trying to get home sir.

PHILOCTETES   Who are you with?

NEOPTOLEMUS   I'm alone.

PHILOCTETES   Are you lying?

NEOPTOLEMUS   No sir.

NAM   He is.

ZULEIKA   He is.

TISHANI   He is.

PHILOCTETES   Are you lying to me?

NEOPTOLEMUS   No sir.

PHILOCTETES takes a long look at him. Drops the arrow.

PHILOCTETES   I used to wear that uniform.
                Long time ago now.

NEOPTOLEMUS   Are you a soldier?

PHILOCTETES   You can't dock boats here.

SHILOH   They'll take you away.

MAGDALENA   They'll be clinging to your mast.

NEOPTOLEMUS   There's a bay. Just round that headland.
                I just moored up.

PHILOCTETES   Have you registered? To land?

NEOPTOLEMUS   I'm not staying, I'm just passing.
                I'm heading home.

[42]

PHILOCTETES   No one's stopped you? Apart from me?

NEOPTOLEMUS   No. Well, I met these women.

PHILOCTETES   Women? That's pushing it.

                Yes, I'm a soldier. I was a soldier. I was
                a very brave soldier. Same uniform. Long
                while since I've seen it.

NEOPTOLEMUS   When did you serve?

PHILOCTETES   Long time ago now. I was wounded.

NEOPTOLEMUS   What's your name?

PHILOCTETES   *(suspicious, hand tightens on bow handle)*
                What's your name?

NEOPTOLEMUS   Neoptolemus.

PHILOCTETES relaxes.

NEOPTOLEMUS   Where did you fight?

ZULEIKA   Here we go.

SHILOH   I love this one.

NAM   He's very good, actually, this kid.

PHILOCTETES   I fought everywhere. All the big battles.
                Most of them twice.

NEOPTOLEMUS   The first campaign?

PHILOCTETES   That was my last. Been stuck here since.
              Wounded. Got this.

NEOPTOLEMUS   My dad fought at that battle.

PHILOCTETES   What's his name then?

NEOPTOLEMUS   You probably don't know him.

NAM   Go on.

PHILOCTETES   I might do.

NEOPTOLEMUS   Achilles.

PHILOCTETES   Achilles?

NEOPTOLEMUS   Yeah.

PHILOCTETES   No!

NEOPTOLEMUS   What?

PHILOCTETES   Achilles?? I *know* Achilles! Your *dad*?!
              He was a friend of mine! A good one.
              He was. Yeah, I remember him. Not one
              for clever talk, just said what he meant.
              You could trust him. A very brave man.
              Wow. I'd almost forgotten. It's been . . .

PHILOCTETES seems weak suddenly.

NEOPTOLEMUS   Are you all right?

PHILOCTETES ignores him. Stands with his hands on his knees getting his breath. Dizzy. Answering a call within. Until he feels more like himself.

PHILOCTETES   Unbelievable, really.

NEOPTOLEMUS   I know! What a coincidence!

PHILOCTETES   You look just like him.

NEOPTOLEMUS

PHILOCTETES   I have a son, about your age. I have a wife. Had. We lived in a house, beautiful house up in the mountains. You could smell the herbs three miles down the track. All seems like another. Like a dream. Not sure where they are now. I sent messages back. Or tried to. But I've never heard anything. So I don't know. If they know I'm alive or anything. He was so young. Little baby when I left. Maybe your age now.

You have a very straight back.

NEOPTOLEMUS   Thank you.

PHILOCTETES   You keep that up. I have a hunch, see? Never used to have it, but I think, because of all the pain, means I slouch. A good posture is very important for self-reliance, really. And for keeping everything working right. The mind as well as the, the spine.

NEOPTOLEMUS   Yes sir.

PHILOCTETES   How's your sight?

NEOPTOLEMUS   Perfect. No problems.

PHILOCTETES   Good. How are your arms? Are they even?

He inspects them.

NEOPTOLEMUS   What was his name?

PHILOCTETES   What?

NEOPTOLEMUS   Your son?

PHILOCTETES   Oh names. Names are hard. Names escape me
now more and more. It's only because you
don't have much call for saying any names
out here. Mine. I have one. But I haven't
heard it in so long. It's just, when you're
fending for yourself like I am, out here,
hunger, pain, sleep, these are the things
you think about, you see? Names of leaves.
I made up names for every root and stem in
these woods. These are the important things.
My name is Philoctetes. My son. I don't
remember his name. Which is very sad.

NEOPTOLEMUS   You're Philoctetes?

SHILOH   He is good, you're right.

NAM   I know talent when I see it.

JELLY   What, is he doing his acting? Now?
I didn't realize.

[46]

NEOPTOLEMUS   The great Philoctetes! It can't be.

PHILOCTETES   *(struck by the sound of his name said out loud)*
I *am*. I was. But now. I'm not so sure, really.
If it wasn't for this.

NEOPTOLEMUS   Is that it? The bow?

YASMEEN   That's it.

TAYIR   The bow!

YASMEEN   The famous bow.

ZULEIKA   The very one.

PHILOCTETES   Hercules gave it me.

NEOPTOLEMUS   You knew him? Hercules?

SHILOH   Oh yeah.

MAGDALENA   Course he did.

JELLY   He knew all them guys.

PHILOCTETES   Oh yeah, I knew all them guys. He was a
good mate of mine. He was in terrible pain
is what it was, and no one would kill him.
But I did. And then he was deified, so it all
worked out really and he gave me this bow.
But I haven't heard from him since. So. He
must be having a good time, being a god.

	I never put it down. It doesn't miss, it draws back in a blink. I can go from seeing the wind move around a bird's wing out the corner of my eye to having it shot out the sky and land at my feet in, what?
JELLY	Two seconds?
PHILOCTETES	Two seconds. It's a good bit of kit. Never been touched by another hand but mine, and his. What's all this about on the run then?
NEOPTOLEMUS	Yes sir. I'm absconded.
PHILOCTETES	Why? What did you do?
NEOPTOLEMUS	No, no, nothing like that – it's more what they did.
PHILOCTETES	Who?
NEOPTOLEMUS	My generals. A bad leader.
MAGDALENA	Go on, what was his name?
NEOPTOLEMUS	Odysseus.
PHILOCTETES	Well, that makes you my enemy's enemy!
ZULEIKA	Amazing!
TAYIR	It must be fate.
NAM	What are the chances?

SHILOH   So, go on then, what happened?

NEOPTOLEMUS When my dad died /

PHILOCTETES   Achilles is dead?

NEOPTOLEMUS He is.

PHILOCTETES   He was good. A good man. A bright light.
                I'm sorry for your loss son. I'm sorry.

NEOPTOLEMUS It's OK. It happens.

PHILOCTETES   No, it's not OK. It's terrible.

*PHILOCTETES seems on the brink of tears. NEOPTOLEMUS is
compelled to comfort him.*

*PHILOCTETES has lost the social requirements for reading
behaviour or playing nice – all his emotions are honest but seem
contrived because of their intensity. He is very comfortable with
silence. NEOPTOLEMUS is not. It all comes spilling out, and he
works himself up to fury.*

NEOPTOLEMUS They came for me in a ship decked with
                garlands. Odysseus and one of the high
                generals. They had the trumpeters and
                everything, the works. They told me that
                now Achilles was dead, it fell to *me*. So,
                of course, I sailed the next day. What else
                could I do? We've always been soldiers in
                my family. It's what I was born for. I have
                to uphold the name. And anyway, I wanted
                to see his body before they burnt it.

But then when I reached the camp the whole
army was just stood there staring at me
saying my God it's Achilles come back to life.

And he was just laid out. So small. The first
time in my life I've ever seen my father in
the flesh, and he's a corpse. So much smaller
than I'd imagined him. Dead cold corpse in
a coffin. I touched him. He was ice cold and
my hand just bounced off him like touching
a wall or a table or something. I didn't cry.
There was nothing there. It was like a cave
just opened up in my chest and pushed all
my organs down into my feet and made this
gaping space. Empty. I thought I would
have felt more honour. More dignity or
something.

I don't know how long I stood there but
eventually I went over to the generals and
I asked for his armour. They said I couldn't
have it. They had given it to Odysseus
and I should go and take it up with him.
I went to Odysseus, he was drinking wine,
surrounded by his men, I walked right up
and asked him. I said, that armour is mine
by right, and Odysseus laughed and said
he was there at the battle and that he had
fought bravely and was loved by my dad
and had been given the armour for what he
had done and he said 'I've been fighting this
war since before you were born, what you
going do with it anyway? Wear it while you
march round the garden?' Everyone laughed.
He spat on the floor by my shoes, very

close to my shoes. I got so angry. I shouted every curse that came into my head. I almost swung for him but a soldier by me stopped my arm, said 'don't risk it' and Odysseus saw that and he laughed at me again and I swear I saw the colour of my skull I was so full of rage and that's when I left. I left the camp, I stole a boat. I ran away. I'll be arrested when they find me. I just didn't know what else to do.

Beat.

PHILOCTETES   Where was Ajax when all this was happening?

NEOPTOLEMUS   Ajax is dead.

PHILOCTETES   Ajax is dead. What about Nestor?

NEOPTOLEMUS   Nestor's alive, but he lost his son. Not been himself since.

PHILOCTETES   Patroclus then? He was like a brother to your dad.

NEOPTOLEMUS   Patroclus is dead.

PHILOCTETES is stunned.

NEOPTOLEMUS   Everybody's dead.

PHILOCTETES   But Odysseus?

NEOPTOLEMUS   Odysseus is alive.

[51]

PHILOCTETES   Ha!

NEOPTOLEMUS

PHILOCTETES   Was always the way. The best ones get
killed. Trust me. All the ones you wish
would stick around. Puff. Never see them
again, can't even really remember what it
felt like to be around them. But the rest of
us stick it out, buried in this shit, up to our
necks in lives we can't stomach. Funny. Sleep
well my Ajax. My Patroclus. It's sad because
I tell you this son, out here, I have, I've
wished for death.

NEOPTOLEMUS

PHILOCTETES   What about Thersites? Very high opinion
of himself, full of hot air. Balloon, we used
to call him. Bet he's doing fine, isn't he?

NEOPTOLEMUS   Thersites made a load of money in oil and
retired to a golf resort.

PHILOCTETES   Course he did. Of. Course. He. Did. Let me
tell you – every man who lies and cheats,
every self-serving greedy maniac just lives
and lives and lives, straight up the greasy
pole for them, while every righteous man
is shot to pieces, double-crossed and left to
rot. But it's *still* better to be righteous, even
wounded, dead or gone insane – you're *still*
better off than those lot: tyrants. Worse.
Braindead bloated gut sick leaders preaching
lies! Pushing their poorly formed opinions

on the rest of us! They're just clods of earth
at the edge of an eroding cliff. I can still hear
them now – proclaiming, judging, sneering
from their high plateaux. But let me tell you
this son, they are all afraid to die.

NEOPTOLEMUS How long have you been on this island?

PHILOCTETES Ten years. Maybe? Hard to be sure. Could
be twenty.

NEOPTOLEMUS Why don't you leave?

PHILOCTETES I was younger then.

MAGDALENA Why doesn't he leave?

JELLY Coz then what would he have?

PHILOCTETES I was so young.

SHILOH Leaving's such a nice idea.

NAM Pin all your hopes on some far place.

YASMEEN Makes the anguish, year on year.

TAYIR Much easier to face.

PHILOCTETES I was so young when he abandoned me here.
I was much stronger then. I could pull a
tree up from the roots with my bare hands.
I could break a branch as thick as your arm
over my bended knee. He took the best years
of my life.

[53]

NEOPTOLEMUS   But what keeps you here?

PHILOCTETES   He took my papers! He tricked me! He didn't
want the men to see it. You have to keep the
blood up when you're fighting. Full of rage.
It's got to be all cause. Start to think about
effect. It's over. We came on land for water.
He lay me down in a cool spot, said 'why
don't you sleep a while in the fresh air?' He
waited till I was out for the count and left
me here to die. I woke up, saw a grey shape
way out near the horizon. Watched that dot
till it wasn't there. That's the last I saw of
him. Can you imagine the pain of that?

NEOPTOLEMUS   Can't you get a ride out on one of those big
black ships?

PHILOCTETES   They're prison ships!

NEOPTOLEMUS   So? Can't they take you?

PHILOCTETES   Without papers?

NEOPTOLEMUS   Have you asked them?

SHILOH   Asked them?

YASMEEN   Never known a trouble in his life this one.

TAYIR   Just ask them nicely!

ZULEIKA   Excuse me sir, I seem to be lost. Can you
help me find my way?

PHILOCTETES   I tell them my story, they don't believe me!
                Course you're Philoctetes, they say, then
                they beat me till I'm bleeding for wasting
                their time. They say nobody comes here by
                accident. Once you're in this muck, you must
                be a criminal and if they treat you like you're
                a certain thing for long enough . . . Few
                times I've tried to get arrested. Thought that
                way, they'd have to write me up. Then I'd
                have my papers!

NEOPTOLEMUS   What did you do?

PHILOCTETES   Attacked an officer one night, downtown,
                where they go to drink.

NEOPTOLEMUS   Did you batter him?

PHILOCTETES   I was very careful actually.

NEOPTOLEMUS   Of course. Sorry.

PHILOCTETES   Fat lot of good it did me.

NEOPTOLEMUS   Why?

JELLY   Not enough beds for the likes of you.

ZULEIKA   Not enough room in the cells.

YASMEEN   Move on before I move you on.

NEOPTOLEMUS   What did they do with you?

PHILOCTETES They dragged me in and hosed me down
and dumped me back out here to die.

NEOPTOLEMUS What's it for? That prison?

PHILOCTETES It's big business.

NEOPTOLEMUS What's it doing here? This island?
What is this place?

PHILOCTETES You don't know?

NEOPTOLEMUS Why would I know?

PHILOCTETES You should know how the world works,
being in the army and everything.

NEOPTOLEMUS No, I am. I'm very up to date.

PHILOCTETES It would seem so.

NEOPTOLEMUS I've never left home before.

PHILOCTETES I see. The cookie thickens.

NEOPTOLEMUS Crumbles.

PHILOCTETES What?

NEOPTOLEMUS The plot thickens. The cookie crumbles.

PHILOCTETES What are you talking about?

NEOPTOLEMUS You said. Nothing.

PHILOCTETES   Don't you get smart with me boy.

NEOPTOLEMUS   I'm not.

PHILOCTETES   I may not know much, but what I know,
               I know well.

NAM   Put that on your banner and take it to battle.

MAGDALENA   Have you seen? The sky is so beautiful today.

PHILOCTETES   It used to be a thriving city. Busy port.
               People everywhere. Bars. Clubs. Music.

SHILOH   Hear him.

NAM   Cheek of it.

TISHANI   Erase us from our own experience.

ZULEIKA   Remember not to mention us at all.

PHILOCTETES   Lots of trade. Full of life! But by the time I
               got dumped, after the civil war, the city was
               demolished. The whole island was in a bad
               way. Then the tornadoes, back to back, just
               ripped the place up. What was left of it.

JELLY   All the same these lot. Like nothing was here
               till they destroyed it.

PHILOCTETES   So, the government, if you could call
               them that, made a deal with some foreign
               investors, built that prison, fortified the
               island, and now it takes inmates from all

over the world, inmates and unrecyclable refuse, and in exchange citizens with the right papers get freedom of movement. Which is why, nobody's here. Apart from the people who work the prison or the rubbish. And most of them get shipped in for it.

NEOPTOLEMUS   What about the women? What are they doing here?

PHILOCTETES   I don't know. I've never asked them.

NEOPTOLEMUS   Don't you have any friends here?

PHILOCTETES   *(giving NEOPTOLEMUS a matey shove)*
I do now! Eh?

NEOPTOLEMUS   So, where do you stay?

PHILOCTETES   In that cave up there.

NEOPTOLEMUS   Looks all right!

PHILOCTETES   All right? It's a cave. It's dark and cold and it stinks of piss.

NEOPTOLEMUS   So, how do you get by?

PHILOCTETES   I kill things and I eat them.

YASMEEN   Rats mostly.

TISHANI   On a good day.

PHILOCTETES	Squirrels, birds sometimes. I do very well. I was the best bowman in the army. I can shoot anything. I've got a chair and a table I made.
SHILOH	Tell him how famous he is. Back home.
JELLY	Tell him he's a hero.
MAGDALENA	Tell him how much he's missed
NEOPTOLEMUS	The story says you died in battle. We've got your portrait on our wine jug.
PHILOCTETES	Well, don't believe everything you make up.
NEOPTOLEMUS	Imagine if you came back? Back from the dead!
TAYIR	I dream of it.
JELLY	I dream of it.
NAM	I dream of it.
PHILOCTETES	I dream of it. Kill Odysseus. Get back home. Then find my family.
NEOPTOLEMUS	We could though! Couldn't we?
PHILOCTETES	Kill Odysseus?
NEOPTOLEMUS	No. I'm going back there. I can take you. If you want?
MAGDALENA	He's good. He's doing it, look.

SHILOH	Too obvious.
NAM	He's never going to fall for it.
ZULEIKA	He might.
PHILOCTETES	You can take me back home?
NEOPTOLEMUS	Yeah! My boat's just over there.
PHILOCTETES	I thought you said it was round that headland?
NEOPTOLEMUS	Oh. Did I? It is.
PHILOCTETES	It is what?
NEOPTOLEMUS	Round that headland.
PHILOCTETES	Why did you point over there then?
ZULEIKA	Oh well. Maybe not.
JELLY	What did I say?
NEOPTOLEMUS	I just got confused, lost my bearings for a moment. In the excitement.
PHILOCTETES	*(suspicious)* Which way is your boat?
NEOPTOLEMUS	It's just over there. I mean, I came from over there, but you can go round, I think, looks like you can go either way. Anyway, I'm sailing home and I can take you with me! Imagine it! The Great Philoctetes! Returns!

PHILOCTETES (*suspicious*) Who are you?

NEOPTOLEMUS Neoptolemus. Son of Achilles. I told you.

PHILOCTETES Why are you here?

NEOPTOLEMUS I told you. Why don't you trust me?

Beat.

PHILOCTETES I'm sorry.

NEOPTOLEMUS Are you crying?

Beat.

PHILOCTETES Do you think she'll recognize me?

NEOPTOLEMUS Who?

PHILOCTETES I was about your age when I left.

NEOPTOLEMUS Your wife?

PHILOCTETES You're not going to sell me off for research
or something?

NEOPTOLEMUS What are you talking about? Nothing like that.

PHILOCTETES I'm sorry I doubted you.

NEOPTOLEMUS It's no problem, really.

PHILOCTETES I've not known any kindness in a very
long time.

NEOPTOLEMUS   Totally understandable. I get it.

PHILOCTETES   I'd forgotten what it feels like, I think,
              to be offered any help.

NEOPTOLEMUS   We need to go.

PHILOCTETES   Go?

NEOPTOLEMUS   It's time. Are you coming?

PHILOCTETES   Yes.

ZULEIKA   I knew it!

MAGDALENA   He's got him!

NAM   Not yet! He's not got him yet.

NEOPTOLEMUS   OK!

PHILOCTETES   OK? OK! Wait . . . I have to.

JELLY   What about your things?

PHILOCTETES   There's a couple of things I need to get from
              the cave. Just a couple of small things.

NEOPTOLEMUS   You sure we can't leave without them?

ZULEIKA   He needs his things.

PHILOCTETES   I need my things. I've lived here a long time.

Beat.

PHILOCTETES   Was a good home. Kept me safe all these years. Warm in the night, cool when the summer came. Got my things where I want them. I know where everything is. Carved a little cup.

PHILOCTETES begins to gather his things into an old sack he finds on the floor: his old bandages, special rocks, bits of apparent rubbish. When NEOPTOLEMUS tries to help, he brushes him away.

PHILOCTETES   Sweat gets in it sometimes, it goes bad. See that yellow in there? Shouldn't be like that, should it? Sometimes I chuck a few maggots in, let them eat the dead flesh off it. Then it really burns. But it's fun to watch. *I* was the bravest soldier in the whole army. Apart from your dad, of course.

TISHANI   Tell him what you could have been!

PHILOCTETES   I could have been a general you see, by now, or maybe the mayor even. Could have built a big house in the town with paintings of my family on all the walls, but he stopped my life short when he left me here.

TAYIR   And how you struggled!

PHILOCTETES   You don't know the struggles I face. He turned me into an animal. He sleeps on silk sheets and drinks the best wine and gets remembered in songs but that should have been my life!

ZULEIKA   And if you were a lesser man.

[63]

PHILOCTETES   If I were a lesser man I'd have given up a
long time ago. But I'll get my revenge, I will.
His time will come. Clear as night. And when
it gets painful, you've no idea, really son,
the pain I'm in. I have to tell you, it's hard
for me. I suffer. You've never known pain,
I hope, like this.

They go into the cave.

*Once they're safely out of the picture, the CHORUS respond
to PHILOCTETES' privileged self-indulgence. They have fun
speaking these lines, they are not lamenting on their misery, they
are taking the piss out of PHILOCTETES.*

AUNTY   Should I list all *my* failings? All *my* pain?
Sit there wailing every minute of the day?
Should I be on my back, arms flailing?
Falling prey to every beast that stalks my
    brain?
Should I be plaything for every pity,
Every craving and every grief that comes
    my way?
Where should I start?

NAM   My broken heart?
I never met a man who stayed.

TISHANI   I've been the other woman now three times.
Each time I gave them everything, they
walked away.

SHILOH   My body's nothing but a grave.
A place I bury every hope I had for love,
or truth or faith.

ZULEIKA   What else?

JELLY   My teeth hurt. My gums are rotten.

YASMEEN   Daughter hates me. Son's forgotten I exist.
               He's addicted.
               Last I heard he'd lost his kids.

JELLY   Hips don't work, I've fucked my back.

NAM   My veins are thick with ancient fat.

SHILOH   I can't walk that post and back.
               Still, I'm on my feet all day.

NAM   Three fractured ribs that never healed.

MAGDALENA   Dizzy spells.

YASMEEN   Achilles heel is swollen.

MAGDALENA   Dad disowned us.
               Everything we had was stolen.

NAM   No sweets or treats or friends for me.

JELLY   All I had was endless grief.

ZULEIKA   They cut my stomach here to here
               And took my unborn child from me.

TAYIR   They tied me up and left me out all night.
               I was a piece of meat.

TISHANI   Happy now?

SHILOH   Are we allowed to get a moment's peace?

PHILOCTETES and NEOPTOLEMUS emerge from the cave,
NEOPTOLEMUS carrying the sack of bandages, a plastic bag full
of weed, an armful of various bits of rubbish, including the chair
PHILOCTETES made. PHILOCTETES carries his bow and is
limping more than before.

NEOPTOLEMUS We better move it.

PHILOCTETES   Why?

NEOPTOLEMUS If we're going to catch the tide.

PHILOCTETES   You look too young to be out there fighting.

NEOPTOLEMUS I'm old enough.

PHILOCTETES   I suppose I was fighting in the big man's
              army at fifteen. Never did me no harm.

NEOPTOLEMUS Have you got everything you need?

PHILOCTETES   First time out, I ducked under, swung
              around, came up from near enough crouching
              and had them on the floor with the back
              of my boot, then I went past at least fifteen
              without getting a scratch on me, put them all
              out, one by one. Bap. Bop. Out. Never looked
              back. I got a medal, cross of the wolf, all that.
              Was one of the best days of my life.

NEOPTOLEMUS We really have to move.

PHILOCTETES   No hurry is there.

PHILOCTETES sits down, looks at things on the floor.

NEOPTOLEMUS Don't you want a lift home?

PHILOCTETES Course I do.

NEOPTOLEMUS So why are you sitting down?

PHILOCTETES Just having a little sit down. The leg.
You know.

NEOPTOLEMUS Well, I'm going.

PHILOCTETES All right then, see you later. I'm just sitting
here for a minute.

NEOPTOLEMUS I'm not going to wait around.

PHILOCTETES Aren't you?

NEOPTOLEMUS Anything could have happened to the ship
by now.

PHILOCTETES You got enough supplies on board?

NEOPTOLEMUS Oh yeah. I've got loads. Got biscuits. Rum.
The lot.

PHILOCTETES I haven't had a biscuit in ages.

NEOPTOLEMUS Plenty on board! And if all else fails, you
can shoot a seagull down, can't you?

PHILOCTETES I could shoot a seagull, I've done it before.

[67]

NEOPTOLEMUS   *(trying to joke)* Tastes like chicken, right?

PHILOCTETES   *(confused)* No.

NEOPTOLEMUS   Come on then!

PHILOCTETES   I'm coming.

He doesn't move, NEOPTOLEMUS changes tack.

NEOPTOLEMUS   It's horrible here.

PHILOCTETES   The worst.

NEOPTOLEMUS   I don't know how you've managed.

PHILOCTETES   Ten years he left me here. I kept myself alive.

NEOPTOLEMUS   Barely.

PHILOCTETES   Barely, you're right. I could have had the finer things.

NEOPTOLEMUS   Does it get lonely?

PHILOCTETES   You don't know the half of it!

NEOPTOLEMUS   What about your wife?

PHILOCTETES   What about her?

NEOPTOLEMUS   What was she like?

PHILOCTETES   Oh. She was. Oh. Well. She was . . .

NEOPTOLEMUS   Bet you'd give anything to see her again?
                Wouldn't you?

PHILOCTETES   I would give anything. A man should be
                with his family.

NEOPTOLEMUS   So, let's go?! Let's go find your family.

PHILOCTETES   Yeah. We're going.

He doesn't move.

SHILOH   He thought he had him there. I can tell.

TAYIR   Stubborn old goat. Bless him.

TISHANI   I know. Smarter than he looks. Sometimes.

YASMEEN   He is what he is, you've got to give him that.

ZULEIKA   I thought the little soldier was doing OK.
                Pretty good liar for someone with all those
                nice morals.

NAM   Moralists make the best liars. Trust me
                on that.

NEOPTOLEMUS   I can't believe it!

PHILOCTETES   What?

NEOPTOLEMUS   Philoctetes!

PHILOCTETES   Me?

NEOPTOLEMUS   My friends are going to lose their minds
              when I tell them!

PHILOCTETES   What are you going to tell them?

NEOPTOLEMUS   About how I met the great man himself!

PHILOCTETES   What will you say about it?

NEOPTOLEMUS   I'll say – he ambushed me, took me by
              surprise and held me at arrow point. And
              I was shitting myself!

PHILOCTETES   You were scared, weren't you? That was
              funny.

NEOPTOLEMUS   He discovered I had a boat and was sailing
              back home and he befriended me so that he
              could jump on board, escape from the island
              he was trapped on and sail home to his wife!

PHILOCTETES   Anything could have happened to her.

NEOPTOLEMUS   And see all his friends again!

PHILOCTETES   I miss my friends.

NEOPTOLEMUS   All the old faces!

PHILOCTETES   They'll cross the road soon as they see
              me coming.

NEOPTOLEMUS   Of course they won't.

PHILOCTETES   Go quiet in the pub when I walk / in

NEOPTOLEMUS   People will come from miles to hear you tell
your / story

PHILOCTETES   They'll only put up with me out of fucking /
manners

NEOPTOLEMUS   Crowds will come to hear you talk in packed
/ rooms

PHILOCTETES   They'll invite me round to their *houses* for
dinner and talk about their politics and their
kid's school and drink their fucking *drinks*
and I'll sit there not knowing where I am or
what / I'm doing

NEOPTOLEMUS   Parties every night, big soft bed to sleep in.

PHILOCTETES begins to feel pulses of pain running through him.

PHILOCTETES   And I'll be sketchy as anything, *(PULSE)*
hear a dog bark or something and I'll stand
up fast, knock the whole table over, and
they'll say it's all right, it's all right, but
when I'm gone they'll laugh, *(PULSE)*
they'll complain about the smell, they'll say
I frighten their wives. No rocks, no palms,
no *(PULSE)* no bush, just big clean cars and
televisions and sitting at home in an empty /
room

NEOPTOLEMUS   A hot bath! Think of it! Deep as a well.
She'll rub your back. The sunlight on the
steam. The feel of her across your / body

[71]

PHILOCTETES They'll send word to her, sure, she'll be shacked up with some modern guy, civilian, *(PULSE)* never shot an arrow in his life. 'He's asking for you again' they'll say and she'll turn and look at her / children

NEOPTOLEMUS They might make you the mayor if you came back! Brand new / life

PHILOCTETES And her husband sitting out in the garden on the fucking *garden furniture*, on the swinging fucking garden chair, and he's *(PULSE)* reading the / paper

NEOPTOLEMUS Be with your family again. You could have grandchildren by / now

PHILOCTETES And their kids are all playing with water balloons in the paddling pool, giggling away. *My* son, my son is all grown up, yeah, playing a bit of fucking cello beneath the *chestnut trees*, in the *afternoon sun*. Cello that his step-dad bought him. And she's listening to him play, some beautiful bit of music and she's thinking *oh for fuck's sake please don't let him fuck up the next ten years of our lives like he just fucked up the last ten. Please don't let him turn my son into a killer. Please God make him leave us alone.*

Pause.

NEOPTOLEMUS What? No. No, it won't be like that.

[72]

PHILOCTETES How much you wanna bet? I go back.
That's my life. Fame and fortune? You're
joking aren't you? It'll only be a matter of
months before they say I'm fit for work and
I'll be out on the high street handing out
fucking CVs – twelve and a half years state-
sanctioned murderer, ten years living in a
cave killing squirrels. My customer-service
skills are, as you can imagine, not quite up
to scratch. *(PULSE)* FUCK.

NEOPTOLEMUS You've got it all wrong. We need you to
come home.

PHILOCTETES THIS IS MY HOME NOW.

PHILOCTETES doubles over and yells in pain and frustration.

NEOPTOLEMUS What's wrong?

PHILOCTETES Nothing. Fine.

NEOPTOLEMUS waits, useless.

NEOPTOLEMUS Is it your leg?

PHILOCTETES begins to pant strangely and clutch himself.

PHILOCTETES This is nothing. I'm fine.

*PHILOCTETES seems to lose control of his faculties, he starts
shaking. Screaming.*

NEOPTOLEMUS *(dropping all the things in his arms)*
What should I do?

[73]

PHILOCTETES   Just STOP THE PAIN. Kill me! I can't take it!
                I can't take it anymore! I give up. THE PAIN.
                I can't. Take. The. Pain. Anymore.

NEOPTOLEMUS reaches out a hand to comfort him.

PHILOCTETES   DON'T TOUCH ME.

*PHILOCTETES grits his teeth, writhing. Stuttering syllables of
pain.*

PHILOCTETES   See the blood? See all that pus? This is what
                it's like. Every fucking TIME.

TAYIR   Take the bow.

SHILOH   He'll never give it.

MAGDALENA   Get it off him.

NEOPTOLEMUS   Shall I take the bow?

PHILOCTETES   What? No! Don't touch it. You won't touch it!

MAGDALENA   Take it.

NEOPTOLEMUS   It's just that you're struggling with it.
                It looks so heavy.

PHILOCTETES   It *is* heavy. It's meant to be heavy.
                It's a burden. A God-given burden.

NEOPTOLEMUS   Let me help you with it.

PHILOCTETES   Never!

[74]

NEOPTOLEMUS I'm not gonna run off with it, am I.

PHILOCTETES screams again and doubles over, shaking the bow.

NEOPTOLEMUS I just want to help you!

PHILOCTETES You can't help me. No one can help me!

JELLY You need to rest.

PHILOCTETES I need to rest. I do.

NEOPTOLEMUS It looks very sore. You've had a shock.

SHILOH You need to get your breath.

PHILOCTETES A big shock. Got to go easy now. Haven't I?

NEOPTOLEMUS Here, sit up, let me . . .

He helps PHILOCTETES sit up, more comfortably.

NEOPTOLEMUS Let me take that, let me hold it for you.

NEOPTOLEMUS reaches for it and they hold it together.

PHILOCTETES AHHGHGGH. KITKAGH. FFFFFARGH. KAKAKAKGHGH. Don't be afraid, this will carry on for a bit. Then I'll pass out. Let me sleep. Don't try and wake me. It's the only relief I get. Just stay by, keep that bow safe, OK?

PHILOCTETES lets go of the bow. When he does, NEOPTOLEMUS moves it further away from his grasp.

TAYIR	He's got it!
SHILOH	I always knew he would.
MAGDALENA	You're very clever.
SHILOH	Am I? Thank you.
MAGDALENA	Yes. You're very clever, and you have an extremely good intuition.
SHILOH	I do, actually. I've been told that before. Thank you.
MAGDALENA	You're welcome. Could you rub my feet?
SHILOH	Nice try.
MAGDALENA	Ahhh go on. Be kind.
SHILOH	I'm not touching your feet!
PHILOCTETES	AGHHHHH! This is *your fault* Odysseus! I wish this life on you, you palace-dwelling shit-stain, unwashed ball-sack of the worst kind. You and your generals. You and all your stinking reptilian paedophile generals. AHHHHHH! Ahh. Ah. KILL ME. Take that bow and shoot me with it if you have a shred of decency in you, you bastard. You fucking bastard boy. Kill me. IT'S HIM THAT DID THIS TO ME. HE PUT ME HERE. HE LEFT ME HERE LIKE THIS.

NEOPTOLEMUS says nothing, watches him. PHILOCTETES has closed his eyes.

PHILOCTETES   Where are you, you little shit?

NEOPTOLEMUS I'm here. I'm here.

PHILOCTETES   Good.

PHILOCTETES settles a bit, smiles heroically through his pain.

PHILOCTETES   It's passing. I'll be back to my old self any
minute.

NEOPTOLEMUS crouches with him. Waiting it out.

PHILOCTETES   Don't leave me, will you?

NEOPTOLEMUS No sir.

PHILOCTETES   Will you guard my bow and stay close by me?

NEOPTOLEMUS Yes sir.

PHILOCTETES   Swear it?

NEOPTOLEMUS wavers.

MAGDALENA   Go on, swear it.

PHILOCTETES   Son?

NEOPTOLEMUS I swear it.

ZULEIKA   You're getting good at lying!

JELLY   You'll be just like the older one soon enough.

[77]

TAYIR	I thought this one was different.
TISHANI	I told you! They're all the same.
SHILOH	It's that heavy name around his neck.
NAM	He doesn't trust anyone, but he trusts you.
YASMEEN	And you trap him with your lies.
PHILOCTETES	Give me your hand.

They shake on it.

PHILOCTETES	AHHH! AHH!

PHILOCTETES slumps into sleep. NEOPTOLEMUS untangles his hand and examines the bow.

TISHANI	You've got the bow.
MAGDALENA	Nicely done.
ZULEIKA	The framework glows as gold as rum.
SHILOH	See – the string.
TAYIR	It sings, the hum.
SHILOH	Of all the things.
NAM	Not yet begun.
TAYIR	Take it.

JELLY	Wait. Doesn't he need *him* and the bow, he can't just take the bow?
NAM	Take it, get back on your boat and leave.
NEOPTOLEMUS	Stop it. Please. I'm trying to /
YASMEEN	Have you ever seen the truth of war? Or just the pictures posted up of bombed-out towns.
TISHANI	Exploded corpses, gross contortions, screaming orphans.
SHILOH	Images make great endorsements, For either side and all their causes.
TAYIR	Uprising or rebel cell or terrorist or infidel.
ZULEIKA	Far-right, far-left or may-as-well-join-up-coz-what-the-hell-my-country's-fucked.
JELLY	You've never seen it, you don't know.
TISHANI	You just imagine, you've been trained.
JELLY	But you've not smelt the guts, the brains.
TAYIR	The insides out, the dead remains.
TISHANI	And you've not known the only hope of violence.
NAM	The last power of your own son's flesh – your enemy is your contrivance, for them, each death brings more respect.

YASMEEN	Is one more step towards an end to all the griefs that live in them.
SHILOH	You turn up here, with your big task, this abstract thing that you've been asked to do.
NEOPTOLEMUS	Shut up.
JELLY	Look at him.
NEOPTOLEMUS	No.
ZULEIKA	You really want to take this man to war?
NEOPTOLEMUS	Leave it. Leave me alone.
NAM	It marked him then.
SHILOH	It marks him now.
YASMEEN	Its mark is on him still.
ZULEIKA	You'd drag him back, the state he's in.
JELLY	And force this man to kill?
TISHANI	This is the glory that you fight for?
NEOPTOLEMUS	Stop it. You don't know anything. I need to /

NEOPTOLEMUS shakes them off. Steels himself for the task at hand and wakes PHILOCTETES.

PHILOCTETES	I thought you would have legged it. Buggered off.

NEOPTOLEMUS I would never have done that.

PHILOCTETES How long was I out?

NEOPTOLEMUS Not long.

PHILOCTETES You sat there by me the whole time?

NEOPTOLEMUS Of course I did.

PHILOCTETES What about the stink? You don't mind the stink?

NEOPTOLEMUS You said to stay by you.

PHILOCTETES *(moved by it)* Fucking hell boy.

NEOPTOLEMUS It comes on like that all the time?

PHILOCTETES All the time, yeah.

NEOPTOLEMUS For a minute there, I thought you were dead.

A flash of menace crosses PHILOCTETES, he rears up at NEOPTOLEMUS.

PHILOCTETES You'd have liked that, wouldn't you?

NEOPTOLEMUS faces it, shaken, until the menace loses its heat.

NEOPTOLEMUS Can you stand?

PHILOCTETES Course I can.

NEOPTOLEMUS Here, take my arm.

They begin to walk towards the beach.

PHILOCTETES   I go into these dreams. When I'm out
like that.

NEOPTOLEMUS What do you see?

PHILOCTETES   Him. Always the same.

*PHILOCTETES picks up a handful of dirt and sand and rubs
the grains into his palms then throws the sand towards the cave
mouth. A ritualistic movement. Something holy to it.*

PHILOCTETES   Do you think it will still be there, my house?

NEOPTOLEMUS Yes. It will still be there. Waiting for you.

PHILOCTETES   And my boy, will he be fighting?

NEOPTOLEMUS Oh yes. He'll be all kitted out. Like me.

PHILOCTETES   So, I won't see him then?

NEOPTOLEMUS If he's at the front, we can go and find him.

PHILOCTETES   I'd like to see him.

NEOPTOLEMUS We could go straight there, now, if you like?

PHILOCTETES   My hand used to sink up to the wrist when
I touched his head. That's how thick his hair
was. Black as soil.

NEOPTOLEMUS We could sail straight to the military
harbour, they'd feed us. Proper meal.

Good scrub. Fresh new clothes. Treat you
for the pain.

PHILOCTETES He was born with one arm shorter than the
other and I used to worry, about how he'd
hold his bow.

NEOPTOLEMUS And when you're all clean and smart and
armed to the teeth, we could head out into
battle. All three of us.

PHILOCTETES Me and him and you?

NEOPTOLEMUS We'd cause all kinds of carnage! Us three!
And that bow!

PHILOCTETES Into battle?

NEOPTOLEMUS They'd be falling like confetti. Us three.
We'd be champions. And after, we'd be
surrounded by people, cheering, raising
their glasses, bowing their heads. But
Odysseus. He'd be alone. Once people
know what he did to you, he'll be nothing.
People will spit at him in the street. We'll
make his name a curse. This will be your
revenge.

PHILOCTETES Lovely story, but I don't think so son.

NEOPTOLEMUS This is how we'll get him. We'll make him
an outcast in his homeland.

PHILOCTETES Nice idea, / but

NEOPTOLEMUS   This is the only way we can pay him back for what he did to us.

PHILOCTETES   Drop it, all right? / Leave it

NEOPTOLEMUS   Why? You'd be famous. Back from the dead! The great champion! He'll be ruined. You never leave a wounded man. That's the first thing they teach you. The soldiers will turn against him, but only when they see you marching on that battlefield, covered in the blood of all their dead enemies.

PHILOCTETES grabs NEOPTOLEMUS by the face.

PHILOCTETES   Why are you so fucking keen for me to go to war?

NEOPTOLEMUS   What? I'm not. I'm just /

MAGDALENA   Suspicious, isn't it?

SHILOH   What's his game?

ZULEIKA   He's trying to force you into something.

TAYIR   He's shaking. Look, he's terrified.

JELLY   I don't think you can trust him.

YASMEEN   Is he working for your enemy?

PHILOCTETES   Who are you working for?

NEOPTOLEMUS   What?

PHILOCTETES	Who sent you here?
NEOPTOLEMUS	No one. I told you.
PHILOCTETES	Did he send you?
NEOPTOLEMUS	No! I've never even met him.
PHILOCTETES	You told me you met him. You said you're on the run from him?
NEOPTOLEMUS	I am. I mean, apart from that one time.
PHILOCTETES	I can smell him all over you.
NEOPTOLEMUS	I'm on my way home.
PHILOCTETES	WHO ARE YOU?
NEOPTOLEMUS	I'm Neoptolemus.

ODYSSEUS enters, unseen. Watches them. Seeing PHILOCTETES again unsteadies him. He swigs from his flask.

PHILOCTETES	No more lies. Time for the truth now. THE TRUTH NOW.
NEOPTOLEMUS	I am telling you the /
PHILOCTETES	Are you working for Odysseus?
NEOPTOLEMUS	No.
PHILOCTETES	*(tightening his grip, etc.)* Are you working for Odysseus?

NEOPTOLEMUS   No.

PHILOCTETES   Are you working for Odysseus?

NEOPTOLEMUS   Yes.

PHILOCTETES   What does he want with me?

NEOPTOLEMUS   We need you to fight with us.

PHILOCTETES   Why did he send you?

NEOPTOLEMUS   I've never done anything like this. I don't even want to be a soldier. I can't stand the fucking army.

PHILOCTETES lets go of NEOPTOLEMUS.

PHILOCTETES   Full of lies! You are full of lies and filthy from it.

NEOPTOLEMUS   I had to. I had to.

PHILOCTETES   Where is he?

NEOPTOLEMUS   You've got to come with me. He knew if he asked you himself, you'd never come.

PHILOCTETES   Give me my bow.

NEOPTOLEMUS   No.

PHILOCTETES   Give me my –

He reaches for it, held out of his way, He squares up to the younger man, who grips the wooden handle and uses it to beat him across the shoulders with it as hard as he can.

PHILOCTETES   Your dad would be ashamed of you.

NEOPTOLEMUS So fucking what? I never even met him.

ODYSSEUS steps into the scene.

ODYSSEUS   *(to NEOPTOLEMUS)* You OK?

PHILOCTETES screams. A howl.

ODYSSEUS   Calm down. It's all right.

PHILOCTETES is grimacing. Roaring. Pure anger.

ODYSSEUS   Come on. Calm down.

PHILOCTETES moves towards ODYSSEUS in rage but without conviction. ODYSSEUS reaches out his hand, edges close and touches PHILOCTETES on his shoulder which seems to electrocute PHILOCTETES.

ODYSSEUS   It's OK. It's me. I've come back to get you.

PHILOCTETES   You killed me.

ODYSSEUS   I didn't kill you.

YASMEEN   Bastard.

PHILOCTETES   Fuck you.

ODYSSEUS	After all these years. There you are.
PHILOCTETES	There you are. You look older.
NEOPTOLEMUS	I tried. I was / trying
ODYSSEUS	What did you think was going to happen?
NEOPTOLEMUS	He was about to come with me, I had it all under control.
ODYSSEUS	ENOUGH. Really, that's enough now.
PHILOCTETES	You left me here to die.
ODYSSEUS	I knew you'd be OK.
PHILOCTETES	OK? My life! You took my / life
ODYSSEUS	We offered them a treaty? Did you hear that? We surrendered!
PHILOCTETES	I'm not listening to you.
ODYSSEUS	Don't be like that. Come on.

ODYSSEUS unties a length of rope which he holds behind his back.

ODYSSEUS	The day came for the signing, all the top brass were there, chief of staff. Patroclus. But they *set us up*. The bastards came to the meeting packed to the teeth with explosives. Everybody's dead.
PHILOCTETES	Good. Fuck them. Fuck all of you.

ODYSSEUS   You're our last hope. You and that bow.

PHILOCTETES   *My* bow. Only *I* can shoot it.

ODYSSEUS   I don't sleep at night either. I hear a siren,
                a door slamming, and that's it. I'm punching
                the walls. Seeing all the dead again. They
                should never have sent us out there.

PHILOCTETES   You sent us out there.

ODYSSEUS   But they've got aftercare now. They've got
                ways of helping.

PHILOCTETES   You left me on my own. Here! Penniless,
                destitute. I killed for you. You don't care
                about what I've been going through.

ODYSSEUS   We can treat the memories. There are doctors
                who can help you.

PHILOCTETES   I don't trust your doctors. They'll fill me
                with cancers just to sell me their drugs.

*ODYSSEUS moves towards PHILOCTETES, the rope behind
his back.*

PHILOCTETES   Give it back to me! Tell him to give it back
                to me?

ODYSSEUS   It's too dangerous. You can't have it back
                until you get to the front.

PHILOCTETES   I'm not going back to the fucking front.

TISHANI	He's not going anywhere.
NAM	Leave him alone.
ODYSSEUS	It's safe. You're safe now Philoctetes.
ZULEIKA	He's got a rope.

PHILOCTETES sees the rope and leaps up, pulling a knife from his waist and holding it up to his own throat.

PHILOCTETES	I'll do it.
ODYSSEUS	You won't.
SHILOH	He will.
PHILOCTETES	I will, I'll do it, then you'll be fucked. I've slit enough throats in my time, believe me. I know what I'm doing.

ODYSSEUS sizes up the situation, each time he moves towards PHILOCTETES, PHILOCTETES pushes the blade closer in.

PHILOCTETES	One step closer and I'll slit yours too.

ODYSSEUS lunges towards PHILOCTETES and grabs him, wrestling the knife out of his grasp. NEOPTOLEMUS' training kicks in and in seconds he has the prisoner restrained, bound with rope and is helping ODYSSEUS put a hood over his head.

PHILOCTETES	*(muffled shouting)*
TAYIR	Let him go!

YASMEEN	Leave him alone!
JELLY	Get off him.
ZULEIKA	Cowards. Disgusting.

The CHORUS advance on the soldiers, NEOPTOLEMUS raises the bow. ODYSSEUS holds the knife he took from PHILOCTETES.

ZULEIKA	Go on then.
JELLY	Touch him again. Touch him one more time and see what happens.
NAM	Leave it. Leave them to it.
MAGDALENA	You don't fool us.
NAM	Come away. It's not worth it.
SHILOH	Don't get involved.
TISHANI	We're not scared.
JELLY	Karma. It's a serious thing, you know.
NAM	Stop it, come back.
JELLY	You'll get yours.

They back away. Pulled by the others.

ODYSSEUS	You let him make a fool of you.
NEOPTOLEMUS	I didn't.

ODYSSEUS   You lost control of the situation. You put
                yourself and the whole country in danger.

NEOPTOLEMUS   I didn't. That's not what happened. I was
                in control.

ODYSSEUS   He's an old man, with a bad leg who hasn't
                seen a fight in years, and you gave him the
                upper hand.

NEOPTOLEMUS   It wasn't like that.

PHILOCTETES starts to moan.

ODYSSEUS   All you had to do was follow my orders.
                But you couldn't even do that.

NEOPTOLEMUS   I did follow them.

ODYSSEUS   What's the matter with you?

NEOPTOLEMUS   I felt for him. That's all.

PHILOCTETES' moaning becomes more desperate.

ODYSSEUS   It's like you want us to lose.

NEOPTOLEMUS   I don't know what happened sir

ODYSSEUS   When I was your age, I / had

*PHILOCTETES is shouting. NEOPTOLEMUS kicks him
repeatedly.*

NEOPTOLEMUS   Shut up!

TAYIR	What are you doing?
ZULEIKA	Stop it.
ODYSSEUS	Ignore them.
MAGDALENA	Leave him!
JELLY	You don't kick a person when they're / down
MAGDALENA	You should be ashamed of yourself.

ODYSSEUS shows the knife. JELLY and MAGDALENA throw themselves at NEOPTOLEMUS regardless but ODYSSEUS pushes them back, they jump on him and he throws them off again with a heavy, painful blow.

SHILOH	Don't get / involved
JELLY	We are / involved
ZULEIKA	No no no no, stop! Stop it. / Leave him!
YASMEEN	Leave them to it, trust / me
NAM	Come back, come away.
TISHANI	I told you they were trouble.
MAGDALENA	He's not well.
ZULEIKA	He has fits.
YASMEEN	He won't want you getting into this.

PHILOCTETES goes into a fit, NEOPTOLEMUS stops kicking him.

ODYSSEUS   What are you doing?

NEOPTOLEMUS   He has fits.

ODYSSEUS   This is ridiculous.

TAYIR   He's hurt!

ODYSSEUS   I thought you were a soldier?

NEOPTOLEMUS   I am a soldier.

ODYSSEUS   You don't deserve the uniform.

NEOPTOLEMUS   AGHHH!

YASMEEN   He's all right. Trust me. He's fine. Leave him.

SHILOH   You're sure?

ZULEIKA   He doesn't look fine?

YASMEEN   He's *fine*. He can handle it. It's not worth
                     getting involved.

ODYSSEUS   It's a good thing your father never lived to
                     meet the man you've grown up to be.

*NEOPTOLEMUS throws himself back into the kicking until
PHILOCTETES stops writhing and is still, NEOPTOLEMUS
pisses on PHILOCTETES. It goes on for an uncomfortable length
of time.*

ODYSSEUS	I'm going to find his arrows. Pick him up and take him to the ship.

Exit ODYSSEUS.

NEOPTOLEMUS vomits.

He begins to drag PHILOCTETES but doesn't get far. He puts him down. Listens to his breathing. Unties him. NEOPTOLEMUS collapses in the corner of the stage, head in his hands.

YASMEEN goes to PHILOCTETES, some of the others follow but she makes it clear she wants to go alone. She cleans his face with water. Rubs ointment into his skin to soothe the bruising. He comes round, sees her. They smile at each other.

YASMEEN	You OK?
PHILOCTETES	Think so. Yeah. I'm OK. You OK?
YASMEEN	Yeah. I'm fine.
PHILOCTETES	I think I've pissed myself.
YASMEEN	
PHILOCTETES	I'm sorry. I don't know what's / happened
YASMEEN	Shhh. It's OK.
PHILOCTETES	He told me I could have a big house with a bathtub.
YASMEEN	You'll be all right, you've had worse.

PHILOCTETES   Much worse.

YASMEEN   You can take a few lumps, can't you?

PHILOCTETES   Kids don't know how to swing a punch
these days.

YASMEEN   I was thinking the same thing myself.

*She stays with him a while, singing softly. He is soothed. Holds
her hand, her wrist, her elbow. NEOPTOLEMUS walks over to
PHILOCTETES. YASMEEN gives them space.*

PHILOCTETES

NEOPTOLEMUS   How you doing? You OK?

PHILOCTETES   Why did you do that?

NEOPTOLEMUS   I had to.

PHILOCTETES   In my bad leg as well.

NEOPTOLEMUS   You shouldn't have threatened us like that.

PHILOCTETES   'Us'.

NEOPTOLEMUS

PHILOCTETES   Very professional the way you jumped into
action there. They never used hoods and
cuffs and that when I was training.

NEOPTOLEMUS   It's a different war now.

PHILOCTETES   Why did you untie me?

NEOPTOLEMUS   I want you to walk of your own free will.

PHILOCTETES   You not scared boy?

NEOPTOLEMUS   No.

PHILOCTETES goes to stand. Doesn't get far. Winces for his leg.

PHILOCTETES   Where's he gone?

NEOPTOLEMUS   He's gone to get your arrows.

PHILOCTETES   In *my* cave? I'll kill him. I need my bow.

NEOPTOLEMUS   I have your bow, I'm looking after it.

PHILOCTETES   You patronising little cunt.

NEOPTOLEMUS   It's for the best.

PHILOCTETES   Why are you doing this?

NEOPTOLEMUS   I have to.

PHILOCTETES   You don't have to. You can just stop.

NEOPTOLEMUS sits down next to PHILOCTETES who is lying with his head on the floor.

NAM   How could he do that to him?

TISHANI   Those lot are capable of anything.

NAM	I don't know why I'm surprised.
TAYIR	Disgusting.
SHILOH	I'm sick of violence.
TAYIR	Come here, come and sit with me. Forget them.

NEOPTOLEMUS takes his jacket off and arranges it as a cushion for PHILOCTETES' head.

PHILOCTETES You don't know what I carry boy. You don't know the first thing about it.

NEOPTOLEMUS You could be important to so many people.

PHILOCTETES I don't give a fuck about people, not the type of people you're talking about, anyway.

NEOPTOLEMUS If I was you, and I had this chance to do something. To be of service like that.

PHILOCTETES Service? I hear people are starving. In your land of hope and glory. Starving. Freezing cold. Sitting in the dark. Can't get on a bus to hand the forms in. Fight for that should I? Get sanctioned and you're five weeks without. At least out here, we're all in the same shit. Back there, I remember it – see a body sleeping in a doorway, and you know they're getting pissed on every night by the city boys at closing time or set on fucking fire in their sleeping bags. What service should I be to that?

NEOPTOLEMUS	Well then come back and change it. Give the people something to believe in again. Don't just let it burn.
AUNTY	It's already burnt. Burnt and reburnt.
NAM	Burnt and reburnt.
JELLY	Burnt and reburnt.
SHILOH	Burnt and reburnt and then ash, and then flames.
ZULEIKA	Feed the deep furnace with all that remains of our strength and our shame at the end of each day.
TAYIR	Pit our pain against all that we hope to attain.
NAM	On the hill, staring down at the bodies, the ground is uneven.
TISHANI	We are what we want.
MAGDALENA	Pushing trolleys down aisles.
ALL	Feed.
MAGDALENA	It's the only requirement.
JELLY	Everything else is denial.
ALL	Smile.

NEOPTOLEMUS   Come with me and fight, one last battle,
               and then go home to an easy life. No more
               struggle, no more fucking cave. No more
               pain. A *life*, in the world, with a family.

PHILOCTETES reaches for his bow, asking for it.
NEOPTOLEMUS is unable to give it.

Exit NEOPTOLEMUS.

Once he's alone, PHILOCTETES collapses further into the ground.
Then drags himself up and begins a laborious scramble across the
beach.

PHILOCTETES   What am I going to do?

NAM   What was that?

TISHANI   A little fly buzzed past my ear I think?

JELLY   A fly.

NAM   Oh, did someone speak?

PHILOCTETES   I'm ruined.

TISHANI   It can't be.

NAM   Is he talking to us?

JELLY   I didn't hear him.

TISHANI   It appears he is.

NAM   An honour. Such an honour.

ZULEIKA   Leave him alone, can't you see that he's hurt?

PHILOCTETES   I'm not hurt.

PHILOCTETES accepts the cup he's offered without gratitude.

MAGDALENA   It's liquorice root and ginger. Good for your
                 throat and your chest.

PHILOCTETES   He's got my bow.

ZULEIKA   You'll get it back.

PHILOCTETES   I'll starve without it. Can't hunt with stones.

MAGDALENA   Starve then.

SHILOH   There's a lot here, apart from what you kill –
                 there's lentils here, and rice grows wild.

NAM   And fruit.

JELLY   One jackfruit will feed you for days.

YASMEEN   Chillies up the hill too.

TAYIR   And that's coffee up there.

MAGDALENA   The little green beans are coffee, look.

ZULEIKA   And there's a whole patch of wild garlic in
                 the scrub behind the jail /

PHILOCTETES   Can't live like that. I need my weapon.

SHILOH	So you're not going to die. Basically. If you just look around.
PHILOCTETES	*(angry, throwing his cup)* I *told* you, I can't eat that! I don't *want* to eat that food!

Beat.

PHILOCTETES	It's nice here.

He is ignored.

PHILOCTETES	Nice set-up you got. For the cooking. Where do you get the wood?
TISHANI	We collect it. All the trees that came up. After the storm.
PHILOCTETES	And the rice? Bags of it?
TAYIR	We've been here a long time.
PHILOCTETES	Long as me?
SHILOH	Forever, feels like.
TAYIR	I was born here.
PHILOCTETES	I don't have supplies like this. It's like a little home.
MAGDALENA	You could be out of here on the next tide.
PHILOCTETES	Never. Not with him.

JELLY	What are you doing?
SHILOH	Why don't you leave here?
PHILOCTETES	Don't want to leave.
TISHANI	What are you afraid of?
PHILOCTETES	Nothing.
TAYIR	I'd give anything to leave this island.
PHILOCTETES	Well, that's not my problem is it? STUPID. Don't know anything about the world.
JELLY	Oh dear, does someone need a rest? Sleepy time? Bye byes in your nap nap?
PHILOCTETES	*(raging)* You want to go and fight, do you? Wouldn't last a minute. If you've seen the things *I've* seen, you'd talk differently. I had to cut men open to save the likes of *you* / from
NAM	Nuh-uh. Stop there. Off you go now. Time for you to leave I think.

PHILOCTETES shuts up, surprised. Realizes the CHORUS are serious. He begins to stand up, overdoing the agony of it. Waiting for them to tell him to stay. They don't say anything. He starts to walk away, excruciatingly slowly. Doing anything he can think of to hesitate.

PHILOCTETES	I'm sorry.
JELLY	There's no such thing as sorry.

[103]

SHILOH	You either do right or you don't do right. There's no use giving it I *will* do better. Doesn't exist.
PHILOCTETES	It was nice sitting down there with you. It's the pain makes me not myself.
TAYIR	Nice words do you no good here.
NAM	Go on, back to your little misery pit.
PHILOCTETES	No! Please let me stay here with you?
TISHANI	Spent a decade damning everything about this place.
JELLY	Wouldn't say a word to us.
TISHANI	Now here's your chance to leave.
NAM	On a silver fucking ship.
JELLY	Total popstar blowjob high life.
YASMEEN	Swish little place in the Maldives no doubt.
MAGDALENA	Summers in Paris.
ZULEIKA	Internationalist.
TAYIR	Borderless.
SHILOH	Existence of a prince.
JELLY	You think we *want* this life?

TISHANI	I lost my house, my possessions, my *child*. Everything is gone. I'm OK. I'm happy.

Laughter. Throughout.

MAGDALENA	Never been happier.
TAYIR	He's offering you a passport! Freedom of movement!
SHILOH	Who cares Odysseus dumped you here all those years ago? You had a nice little break from the war. Learnt a thing or two, didn't you – really got to know yourself.
MAGDALENA	Really saw the world.
JELLY	Holistic retreat. Raw food diet. Hunter-gatherer experience.
NAM	Just need a backstreet colonic and you've got the full package.
TAYIR	You'll go back beaming.
JELLY	Never shot *me* no rabbits.
YASMEEN	That bow makes you too proud.
MAGDALENA	She's right.
YASMEEN	Losing that bow could be the best thing that ever happened to you.
TISHANI	You could start again.

TAYIR	Give up gluten.
NAM	Practice yoga.
TISHANI	Drink more water.
PHILOCTETES	I need herbs. I've got to smoke something. My leg. My fucking LEG.

PHILOCTETES slumps back towards his cave. MAGDALENA brings AUNTY a cup of tea, wraps her shawl a little tighter round her.

YASMEEN	Life and soul of the party, isn't he?
NAM	Still, nice he stopped by.

ODYSSEUS, collecting arrows on the other side of the beach, sees NEOPTOLEMUS.

ODYSSEUS	Where is he?
NEOPTOLEMUS	He's where we left him.
ODYSSEUS	What are you doing?
NEOPTOLEMUS	Getting water.
ODYSSEUS	For him?
NEOPTOLEMUS	I think he needs a sip of water.
ODYSSEUS	Is he secure?
NEOPTOLEMUS	Of course he is.

ODYSSEUS   And you?

NEOPTOLEMUS Yes sir. I'm fine.

He clearly isn't.

ODYSSEUS   Do you know how he got that wound?

NEOPTOLEMUS No sir.

ODYSSEUS   We were clearing a province, we'd been off
the base for days. We had intel, there was
supposed to be an elite squad. We got to
this village, all the houses had been blown
to bits and there were these children, three
very young children, just sitting there,
watching. It doesn't do them any good to
cry so they're not crying, they're just sat
there in the rubble where the village used
to be. It chilled me to the bone. He was
playing to the troops, giving it the big
performance. He'd got it into his head that
the enemy were in this building at the back
of the square and I was saying, breathe,
stay low, wait for my signal, but I couldn't
even get to the end of my sentence, he just
ran out there in front, he blew our cover
and his own leg to bits. So, of course, we go
in to carry him out of there, and they're on
us. They are fucking on us. I lost six of my
best in that square. And those little kids
didn't make a sound the whole time. He
didn't care about any of us. His selfishness
killed six of his own.

ODYSSEUS takes out his flask, not hiding it anymore, and swigs deep before offering it to NEOPTOLEMUS who declines. He offers again, this time he accepts.

> As soon as it happened, he was telling me I'd done it to him. *You should never have had me out there. I'm your best asset. I could have won this war on my own. This isn't my fate. You've ruined my life.*

Beat.

> Do you know how long it's been since I've seen *my* family?

NEOPTOLEMUS   No sir.

ODYSSEUS   Same goes for all of the troops who were on board with us.

NEOPTOLEMUS   But how could you leave him? A wounded man. Your friend.

ODYSSEUS   He was not a wounded man. He was not my friend. He was a mechanism in an intricate machine. Like we all are. He was broken, and he became dangerous. The smell of the wound was so bad that people were getting ill. Of course I didn't want to leave him. He was draining us. Always complaining. People were losing the will to continue. He was oblivious of course, screaming his head off all night and day. No one could sleep. It was the hardest thing I ever had to do. And I'd do it again.

NEOPTOLEMUS   I don't think he's able to fight. I think
               the man you knew before is not the man
               I've met.

ODYSSEUS   You've been caught up in his fine talk.

NEOPTOLEMUS   No sir.

ODYSSEUS   He has no morals. He's a hypocrite! Sit in
               your filth blaming the world, nothing will
               change.

NEOPTOLEMUS   He lives in a cave, he has no friends, he has
               to kill rats to survive. Please sir.

ODYSSEUS   When I step out to battle I take full
               responsibility.

NEOPTOLEMUS   You would not have lasted ten years out
               here alone.

ODYSSEUS   He has you.

NEOPTOLEMUS   He has me. You have me. The army has me.
               My mother has me. I'm ready to die for the
               cause. I'm ready to slaughter. But I don't
               want to drag this man bound and gagged to
               a warzone and unleash him on himself in the
               middle of a screaming battle.

ODYSSEUS   What a time to be alive.

NEOPTOLEMUS

ODYSSEUS   When I was your age, there was nothing like
              this. It must make it hard to know where you
              stand.

NEOPTOLEMUS   I know exactly where I stand.

ODYSSEUS   Doesn't it all feel pointless sometimes?

NEOPTOLEMUS   I love my country.

ODYSSEUS   Doesn't it feel there's nothing left to fight for?

NEOPTOLEMUS   I was born to fight this battle.

ODYSSEUS   Don't you wish you could just give up?

NEOPTOLEMUS   No! I'll never surrender. I'll fight till the end.

ODYSSEUS   Doesn't it feel like your father's name is a
              weight you cannot carry?

NEOPTOLEMUS   I'm proud of my family.

ODYSSEUS   Aren't you dizzy from standing on the
              shifting edge of such a terrifying change?

NEOPTOLEMUS   They want us all dead.

ODYSSEUS   You could just let him go. And we could
              leave. And that could be it.

NEOPTOLEMUS   We can't do that.

ODYSSEUS   No.

NEOPTOLEMUS   We can't let this be the end.

ODYSSEUS   Get him on the boat.

Exit ODYSSEUS.

NEOPTOLEMUS steels himself for it, then approaches the cave.
PHILOCTETES is singing to himself inside. An old military song.

NEOPTOLEMUS   I've got you some water.

PHILOCTETES   I've got water.

NEOPTOLEMUS   Are you feeling all right?

PHILOCTETES   Fuck off.

NEOPTOLEMUS   I know you must be, must not know what
              to make of any of this, I can see that you
              must / be

PHILOCTETES   What do you want?

NEOPTOLEMUS   I brought you back your bow.

NEOPTOLEMUS holds out the bow.

NEOPTOLEMUS   Please listen to me.

PHILOCTETES takes it.

NEOPTOLEMUS   I did the right thing, I gave it back to you.
              I honoured our friendship. Now you do the
              right thing.

PHILOCTETES	Parade me up and down like some fucking toy monkey. I don't want it. I like it / here
NEOPTOLEMUS	We can't do this without you.
PHILOCTETES	False cities with all their false talk of freedom and / democracy
NEOPTOLEMUS	Please trust me.
PHILOCTETES	I trust it here. I trust the weather. When it says I'm gonna fuck you that's exactly what it means.
NEOPTOLEMUS	How can you have it on your conscience?
PHILOCTETES	It's not on my conscience. It's on his.
NEOPTOLEMUS	Why can't you just listen?
PHILOCTETES	It's *you* not listening! It's *you* not seeing!
NEOPTOLEMUS	Fuck Odysseus. Fuck the mission. Fuck this island, all of it, the whole story. I'm talking me to you. Straight up. Please! For the future.
PHILOCTETES	Why should I fight for something that is already lost?
NEOPTOLEMUS	Think about the bigger picture!
PHILOCTETES	There is no bigger picture! There's this island, from that driftwood down there, to the rocks beyond that headland. That is the picture in its entirety.

NEOPTOLEMUS   You told me you missed it! You said you
              wanted to go / home

PHILOCTETES   I never said that!

NEOPTOLEMUS   You did, I remember, you said exactly / that

PHILOCTETES   I hate the place.

NEOPTOLEMUS   You had a lovely house in the mountains,
              you said, you could smell the herbs from
              miles / away

PHILOCTETES   You're twisting my words. You people always
              do that. That's exactly what people like you
              do. Twist up my words till I can't / think

NEOPTOLEMUS   You're a grown man for fuck's sake.

PHILOCTETES   I don't *know* what I said or what I didn't say.
              I'm not going back.

NEOPTOLEMUS   But you wanted to come with me in my ship?
              We were about to leave?

*PHILOCTETES can't take it, the pressure of the conversation is
too much. He screams in frustration and covers his head with his
hand, he begins to rock, as if about to go into another fit.*

NEOPTOLEMUS   Stop, stop that . . .

PHILOCTETES doesn't.

NEOPTOLEMUS   Please. Calm down.

PHILOCTETES starts to cry.

NEOPTOLEMUS Don't cry.

*NEOPTOLEMUS goes to him and comforts him. As he gets close,
PHILOCTETES grabs him in a hug. Clings to him.*

PHILOCTETES   I thought you were telling the truth.

NEOPTOLEMUS I'm sorry I lied to you.

PHILOCTETES dries his eyes, but is still shuddering.

JELLY   Just let the man rest now, come on.

NAM   Let us rest more like. I've been listening to
                   this nonsense since daybreak.

TAYIR   This is my chance. I'm sorry but I'm going
                   with them.

JELLY   You're going with who?

TAYIR   Don't you see? He's got a boat! I'm getting
                   on that boat, and I'm gone.

ZULEIKA   I want to go.

TAYIR   I'm going alone.

ZULEIKA   You can't just leave me.

JELLY   If they find you at the border, they'll put
                   you in the jail, no trial. You'll be stuck there.
                   Years could pass.

TAYIR   Not me. It won't be like that for me.

JELLY   I was fourteen years in a camp, waiting for
             status. And they still sent me back. You're
             better off here, with us. Trust me.

TAYIR   I can't live another year holding all this in.
             I have to try and find him. If I die I die. I'm
             going to die anyway. I may as well die out
             there, looking for a better life. Rather than
             just sit here and wait for my time to run out.
             This is my chance.

ZULEIKA   I don't want you to get hurt.

NEOPTOLEMUS We can't just sit here and wait for our
             time to run out. If we don't do something,
             everything will be lost.

PHILOCTETES I said: everything's lost already.

NEOPTOLEMUS No it isn't!

PHILOCTETES It's just emptiness! Emptiness at the expense
             of emptiness to increase emptiness for the
             pursuit of emptiness and you can see it in
             everyone's eyes. Our country is nothing
             more than a cradle for tyranny. In her cities,
             the mean-spirited coward gains the world,
             and integrity is punished with despair. You
             want me to go and fight? Unholy, unhumble,
             unaware, unappreciative, unthankful,
             unkind, undone. Too selfish. Emptiness and
             echoes. Even if we do go back and save the
             day, the mess just deepens and worsens,

and we end up fooling ourselves into
fascism, out of fascism, back into fascism
under a different name, into genocide, out
of genocide, back into genocide under a
different name and into the most damaging
era of existence propped up by grandiose
concepts that have no real worth and false
economies built on manufactured insecurity,
anxiety and illness and the rampant
oppression of people based solely on skin
colour which has carved a welt into the
fabric of the world that will not be healed
as long as it can be ignored. I've seen it, I
drank the black water that gathers in the
vines, I got the visions – all the heroes fall to
the superficial nothing-life, living into the
blindness for so long that they succumb to
the blindness and enjoy the blindness and
imagine themselves to be full of integrity.
I've seen the future. There is no grace in
death, people live forever, bloated on their
hatred, screaming out to close the borders,
stockpile the medication, trading pixelated
sexual favours with other people's avatars.
I've seen it. I drank the black water. There
is no glory in our country to fight for. Our
country is Hell. And the terrified, distracted,
just-getting-on-with-it, I'm-not-to-blame-
so-don't-ask-me-to-change people are the
demons who serve in her furnace.

NEOPTOLEMUS What do you want me to do?

PHILOCTETES Go away so it's like you never came. Leave
me here. With my bow. So I can be myself.

NEOPTOLEMUS When they win they will kill your son.

PHILOCTETES My son was born dead like the rest of us. He'll be all right.

Enter ODYSSEUS.

PHILOCTETES sees him, and before ODYSSEUS can respond, he has reached for two arrows from a pouch on his body and raised his bow in a fluid, expert movement. NEOPTOLEMUS grabs PHILOCTETES arm. PHILOCTETES tries to shake him off but he holds on. PHILOCTETES lets loose the arrows, he misses the heart but they root deep in ODYSSEUS' leg. They split the flesh away from the bone creating a gaping hole.

ODYSSEUS drops to the floor in the corner, his leg a mess and crawls offstage.

NEOPTOLEMUS stops PHILOCTETES from launching another arrow, throwing his entire body into disarming him.

PHILOCTETES Ten years I waited for that moment! Over and over, I played it over and over in my head. And you ruined it!

He raises his arrow and levels it at NEOPTOLEMUS.

NEOPTOLEMUS Nobody wins.

PHILOCTETES If your old dad could see us now.

NEOPTOLEMUS He believed in things! In his *country*.

PHILOCTETES He didn't give a fuck about the country. He believed in his wage. In providing for you.

NEOPTOLEMUS   Well that's still something.

PHILOCTETES   He'd be turning in his grave.

PHILOCTETES stares down the shaft of his arrow at NEOPTOLEMUS

NEOPTOLEMUS   I'm trying to help you.

PHILOCTETES   I don't need your help. *You* need *my* help.

Beat.

>That'll bleed out pretty bad. He'll be in agony with that. You better go and see to him.

NEOPTOLEMUS runs for his general.

PHILOCTETES waits to feel grandly different. Better. But is unchanged. He finds YASMEEN, they are alone.

YASMEEN   You all right?

PHILOCTETES   I wanted that for so long.

YASMEEN   You don't feel good?

PHILOCTETES   I don't feel anything.

YASMEEN   Treat violence with violence
and rewound the wounded
and rewind the memories
and refill the emptiness
and refuel the terror
and replay the rage,

and it will keep you as small
as the battles you wage.

PHILOCTETES   I miss home.

YASMEEN   I know you do.

PHILOCTETES   But I'm not the same. Home doesn't exist
               anymore. It probably never existed.

YASMEEN   It's been a long day. Don't get too wound up,
               OK?

PHILOCTETES   I don't want to fight those men. I don't hate
               them. Why should I kill them?

YASMEEN   Try not to go too far into the spin? You
               understand me? Try and stay on top of it?

*YASMEEN encourages him to breathe deeply. PHILOCTETES
notices her body and is moved. They push close, energy rises
between them.*

PHILOCTETES   Yasmeen.

YASMEEN   Philoctetes.

PHILOCTETES   Yasmeen.

YASMEEN   Philoctetes.

Beat.

PHILOCTETES   Come with me?

YASMEEN   Excuse me?

PHILOCTETES   I mean, would you like to, please, come
                 with me?

Beat.

YASMEEN   Why would I leave?

PHILOCTETES   I'll look after you.

YASMEEN   It's me looks after you Phil.

PHILOCTETES   Well, you look after me then. Fine.

YASMEEN   And what, be your mistress?

PHILOCTETES   No.

YASMEEN   Yes.

PHILOCTETES   It won't be like that.

YASMEEN   Thank you, really. Thank you. But I'm
                 happy here. I'll stay with my sisters.

PHILOCTETES   You won't come?

YASMEEN   No. You go.

PHILOCTETES   I don't even know if I want to.

YASMEEN

PHILOCTETES   What?

YASMEEN   Nothing.

PHILOCTETES   What? Why did you make that face?

YASMEEN   Don't get angry.

PHILOCTETES   I'm not angry.

PHILOCTETES gives YASMEEN the bow.

You have it.

YASMEEN

PHILOCTETES   I'm not Philoctetes. Philoctetes is a story
people tell about a man that never lived.
I'm not him. I've never been him. Please.
You have it.

YASMEEN   And do what with it?

PHILOCTETES   Anything you want.

YASMEEN

PHILOCTETES   I should have waited for his word that day.
Instead of just running out like that. I was
blind. Too impulsive, proud, hungry . . . for
the glory. People died.

YASMEEN

PHILOCTETES	I don't want to carry it around forever.
YASMEEN	You left as a great warrior. You'll go back as a refugee.
PHILOCTETES	Maybe so.
YASMEEN	Without your bow, you'll be nameless.
PHILOCTETES	There's things I want to know that I can't know when I'm holding that.
YASMEEN	
PHILOCTETES	Come with me? We could make it an adventure.
YASMEEN	If I come with you, you won't learn anything new.
PHILOCTETES	I could get a normal job.
YASMEEN	Not without your papers.
PHILOCTETES	We could buy a little car.
YASMEEN	It would drive you over the edge that life. And me too.
PHILOCTETES	We could be together.
YASMEEN	That's not what I want.
PHILOCTETES	What do you want?

YASMEEN   I want to sit by the fire and watch the sun
                 go down.

PHILOCTETES

YASMEEN   I don't need to be getting on some boat
                 going God knows where to start a new life of
                 what? Soothing your troubles and cleaning
                 your pants? My life is here. Maybe I'll see
                 you when they bring you back and dump
                 you on the sand again.

PHILOCTETES   Can't you just let me be right? Just
                 sometimes?

YASMEEN   You want to take someone, take Tayir.

PHILOCTETES   I've never even spoken two words to the girl.
                 Why would I take her?

YASMEEN   She might make a life of it, you never know.
                 People do.

PHILOCTETES   Where do I take her?

YASMEEN   Just wherever you're going. To the mainland.

PHILOCTETES   We could have our own rooms?
                 Our own / space

YASMEEN   You're only saying all this because you don't
                 know how to say thanks for whatever it was
                 we shared and goodbye. But that's what you
                 want to say. That's what I want to say.

PHILOCTETES   I'll look after her.

YASMEEN   She can look after herself.

PHILOCTETES   OK. But still. I'll look after her. Tell her to
               pack her things. I'll wait for her in the boat.
               But I won't wait long.

They kiss.

PHILOCTETES   We had a good time, didn't we?

YASMEEN   Yeah, sometimes.

PHILOCTETES   Not sometimes.

YASMEEN   When it was nice, it was nice.

PHILOCTETES   I'm sad to leave you.

YASMEEN   You make me smile.

PHILOCTETES   I don't want to be angry all the time.

YASMEEN

PHILOCTETES   It's like I'm two people, and I don't know
               which one is the real one.

YASMEEN   This one is the real one.

*PHILOCTETES returns to his cave. YASMEEN sits with TAYIR,
whispering into her ear.*

NEOPTOLEMUS helps ODYSSEUS back onto the beach near the CHORUS. His leg is wounded and bleeding. He is stuffing damp sand into it. Trying to stop the bleeding with ripped-up plastic bags.

NAM   You need raw garlic. It's antiseptic. And oregano, it's a natural antibiotic.

ODYSSEUS   I'm not a fucking pizza, am I?

SHILOH   And this oil. You need to rub it in. It will clot the wound.

ODYSSEUS   Leave me.

NAM   You've lost a lot of blood. Look. It split the flesh there.

MAGDALENA   It's not clean. It's full of sand. You need to clean it.

ODYSSEUS   Leave me alone.

SHILOH   You'll die.

ODYSSEUS   No chance.

NEOPTOLEMUS begins to clean the wound with water, rips his shirt to make a tourniquet. Mechanical movements, straight out of a training operation. But his hands are shaking.

ODYSSEUS   Good, that's right.

NEOPTOLEMUS   The flint, there's still bits, some bits are still in there.

ODYSSEUS   Pull them out then.

NEOPTOLEMUS   With my hands?

ODYSSEUS   No, with your feet.

NEOPTOLEMUS   And then, like this. With the cloth?

ODYSSEUS   And pull it tight.

NEOPTOLEMUS   What do we do? Do we storm the cave?

ODYSSEUS   No.

NEOPTOLEMUS   I thought – I thought if he had the bow
              back, it would remind him, who he was.

ODYSSEUS   Well, congratulations on another excellent
              initiative.

NEOPTOLEMUS   We should leave now, shouldn't we?

ODYSSEUS   If I don't make it back, when they ask you
              what happened, make it a better story than
              it was? OK?

NEOPTOLEMUS

ODYSSEUS   Tell them how fierce I was until the end.
              That my last words were something
              profound, you know, bordering on nonsense.

NEOPTOLEMUS   There's no way you're not getting off this
              island, the prophet said we'll be heroes.

ODYSSEUS   I abducted that prophet. Starved them half
                  to death. Tortured them till they had no
                  choice but to tell me what I wanted to hear.

NEOPTOLEMUS You tortured the prophet?

ODYSSEUS   I was looking for names, double agents,
                  terror cells. Thinking about it now, was a
                  pretty good stunt they pulled sending us on
                  this fucking goose chase.

NEOPTOLEMUS makes a gesture of penitence.

NEOPTOLEMUS Forgive us. Forgive us.

ODYSSEUS   Repatriate the pariah, they said. Bring the
                  reluctant hero to the front and victory is
                  yours. I wanted to impress the generals,
                  boost the troops. So off I went, to save the
                  day as usual. I've only myself to blame.

NEOPTOLEMUS

ODYSSEUS   Watch out for pride, it's a terrible engine.
                  And once it gets going, it pushes and pushes.

NEOPTOLEMUS goes to the camp and asks the CHORUS.

NEOPTOLEMUS Can you help us? Can you help my friend?

YASMEEN   Does your friend want help?

ODYSSEUS   No.

NEOPTOLEMUS   Yes, he does. Something for the pain maybe?

ZULEIKA   Give him this tea.

ODYSSEUS   I won't have it. I won't drink that muck.
It's poison.

JELLY   The dogs will come after that wound once
the sun goes down.

ZULEIKA   You need to get it raised up.

TISHANI   I have bandages and antibacterial, from
the clinic.

NAM   I wouldn't waste it on him.

ODYSSEUS   I don't need it. I don't need any help.
I can figure this out. I've been through
worse than this.

NEOPTOLEMUS   What are we going to do?

ODYSSEUS   Let me just. I'm thinking, will you just give
me a second please, to think.

NEOPTOLEMUS   Let's just leave. Fuck the orders.

ODYSSEUS   *Fuck the orders*?

NEOPTOLEMUS   Yes sir. Sorry / sir

ODYSSEUS   Go and get some firewood. I'll make a shelter
no problem and I'll sort this mess out for the
both of us. Again.

NEOPTOLEMUS leaves.

JELLY   I remember you from when you came before,
       with him. To leave him.

ODYSSEUS   You don't remember me.

JELLY   What happened to you? You were much
       nicer then.

ODYSSEUS   I've never seen you before.

JELLY   Left him asleep on the beach. For your
       generals, you said. And now you come back,
       for your generals again.

ODYSSEUS falls into a sleep.

       Don't sleep. Not now. Come on. What's your
       wife's name? What's your home town called?

He doesn't know.

JELLY   How many kids do you have?

MAGDALENA Don't sleep, no, wake up.

ZULEIKA   Go and wake him up.

ODYSSEUS   They'll tell my story.

JELLY   Yes, course they will my love. Of course
       they will.

ODYSSEUS   I never gave up.

NAM   No, you were very brave.

*He is weak, immobile, but breathing steadily. TAYIR is getting
ready to leave, packing things carefully into a battered backpack.
JELLY and NAM watch ODYSSEUS for a sad while. They empty
his pockets. Find a packet of fruit pastilles, which they begin to
eat. Some identification documents, some cash. A little notebook
and a pencil. A pair of reading glasses which they give to AUNTY
to try on. She looks through them, still blind. ODYSSEUS tries
to complain but they shush him and he submits. ZULEIKA joins
them, takes ODYSSEUS' jacket off and tries it on. Does it up
around her and enjoys the fit. NAM comes and takes his boots.
Puts them on her hands and admires the soles. YASMEEN takes
off the armour, leaves it on the sand.*

*NEOPTOLEMUS is carrying a dry pallet, a tarp and some
newspaper.*

NEOPTOLEMUS I found these! I'll get a fire going . . . why
             are you wearing his jacket?

ZULEIKA   He gave it to me.

NEOPTOLEMUS Did you?

ZULEIKA   Peace offering.

*PHILOCTETES emerges from his cave, he stops at the camp and
takes two rabbits from his belt, hands them to JELLY.*

NEOPTOLEMUS What are you doing?

PHILOCTETES Boat's just round that headland.

NEOPTOLEMUS What? Wait? Where are you going?

PHILOCTETES　Home.

NEOPTOLEMUS　What? I thought you said . . .

NEOPTOLEMUS watches as PHILOCTETES walks past him.

NEOPTOLEMUS　Are you going to the war?

PHILOCTETES　No.

NEOPTOLEMUS　Wait!

PHILOCTETES　Why?

NEOPTOLEMUS　I don't want to go either.

PHILOCTETES　Don't go then.

NEOPTOLEMUS　I can't just not go.

PHILOCTETES　Sometimes you've got to disappoint people.

NEOPTOLEMUS　Easy for you to say that. You've got no one to be responsible for. I have to hold the family up. It's just me and Mum. She's not. She doesn't take well to. And the army needs me. And the whole fucking . . .

PHILOCTETES　Sometimes you have to destroy yourself.

NEOPTOLEMUS　I'm burning up.

PHILOCTETES　What's wrong?

NEOPTOLEMUS　My head, that's all. It's pounding.

PHILOCTETES   It's the fumes, it'll pass.

NEOPTOLEMUS Can I come with you?

PHILOCTETES   You can do what you want.

NEOPTOLEMUS I can't leave him.

PHILOCTETES   Don't leave him then.

NEOPTOLEMUS But what will I do?

PHILOCTETES   Don't eat the pigs. They're radioactive.

NEOPTOLEMUS But /

PHILOCTETES   If you try and bring him to the ship I'll
                    kill him. You too if you're in the way.

*PHILOCTETES walks towards the ship, stopping to pick up
large flat stones from the floor and gradually gathering an armful.
NEOPTOLEMUS rejoins ODYSSEUS and the CHORUS.*

*PHILOCTETES kneels and builds a temple of the stones, one on
top of the other, very slowly. Once it's built he lowers his head to
the ground and prays before it.*

*TISHANI brings a poultice she has made of herbs and begins to
paste it on ODYSSEUS' leg.*

ODYSSEUS   Leave me.

TISHANI   I'm not touching you.

She continues her work. Speaks to NEOPTOLEMUS.

TISHANI   What are you going to do then?

NEOPTOLEMUS *(to ODYSSEUS)* You'll be all right, you'll think of something.

NEOPTOLEMUS begins to leave, after PHILOCTETES, sees the armour on the sand. Stops, picks it up. Puts it on.

The CHORUS go back to tending the fire and preparing the evening meal. TAYIR has her things together. She is held by MAGDALENA.

MAGDALENA   I miss you already.

ZULEIKA approaches and gives TAYIR ODYSSEUS' jacket, which prompts them all to give small offerings. TAYIR goes to AUNTY and falls into her arms, a maternal embrace.

MAGDALENA, TISHANI and NAM drag ODYSSEUS closer to the fire. He pushes them off and gets up.

ODYSSEUS   I can stand up fine.

MAGDALENA   Suit yourself.

ODYSSEUS decides to find a place to sleep for the night. Gathers the water and wood and begins to climb up to the cave. He enters the cave.

NEOPTOLEMUS sees PHILOCTETES praying, picks up the tarp from the ground and jumps on him, smashing him on the head with one of the rocks from the stone tower. He throws the tarp over him, secures it, and drags the unconscious body laboriously off stage, towards the ship. It is painful to watch.

TAYIR   Wait!

[133]

TAYIR helps him carry the body.

TAYIR   Like this, don't drop his head. Careful with his leg.

They carry PHILOCTETES off stage.

The CHORUS busy themselves until at last there is peace; the sound of the waves, evening birdsong, the fire.

SHILOH   *(dawns on her)* I've got some rice!

MAGDALENA   Go nice with the tomatoes.

NAM   We've got green tomatoes and yellow tomatoes and purple tomatoes!

TISHANI   Such a nice fire.

JELLY   Never gets old does it, looking at a fire?

YASMEEN   Paradise.

MAGDALENA   Paradise.

SHILOH   Paradise.

YASMEEN   Is there cigarettes?

SHILOH   Here.

SHILOH looks through the things they took from ODYSSEUS, finds tobacco. She passes it to YASMEEN, who begins to roll.

YASMEEN   Thank you.

TISHANI	I've got green peppers.
SHILOH	What happened to those beans in the end? Did we finish them?
NAM	I thought there was some left?

YASMEEN takes the bow to AUNTY. Lights her cigarette and puffs slowly.

YASMEEN	Aunty, what shall we do with this?
JELLY	What do you want to do with it?
ZULEIKA	We don't need that thing.
NAM	It could be useful.
SHILOH	Having a thing like that around will just get us into trouble.
MAGDALENA	We don't need more violence here.
NAM	It could make us powerful.
TISHANI	We're already powerful.
JELLY	It's your call. Whatever you want to do.
ZULEIKA	Sun's setting Aunty! Sun's setting.

AUNTY stands up, adjusts her new glasses.

AUNTY	Big yellow disc in the distance, sinking To blink new light on some other sea, other land.

These are the days.
Let us sleep well and wake to your rays.

Thanks be to the soil and the sea
For the food, the tobacco, the tea.

Another man stranded,
Dug down deep in his cave.
Will there always be one here, lost in his pain
To remind us of how the sum world is
    indifferent?
We take the lessons in hand.

Old blood worked this land many rains back.
It was a fertile place, no waste then.
I ask the grandmothers to watch us this
    evening
And keep us in safety
And hasten to wake us
If something unclean comes into our space
    to debase us.
We trust the island that sustains us.

We ask that the prisoners dream something
    comforting.

We ask that the old goat wakes in the boat
And gets home,
Or at least gets where he's meant to go.
We ask that the waves don't turn them to
    water.
We beg safe passage for our brave daughter.

ALL   Let her be safe.

AUNTY   Give courage. Take courage.

We welcome the spirits of moonlight
   and shadow
To dance in our embers.
Come drink what you find in our stores
Nothing is ours and not yours.

But please grant us the strength
To wake in the morning
In sound mind and body.
Intent to continue.

This island screams and screams all night.
Her head is fire, her chest is tight,
Her teeth are expired dynamite.
Her nails are blunt, her figure slight.
A shadow of her former might.

They come and go, ignore her plight.
Talk like they were born to fight.
It's nothing new, she knows she's right.
Straw fires burn up nice and bright
But fade like candles in sunlight.
It's nothing new. She knows she's right.
This island screams, and screams all night.
Her head is fire, her chest is tight.

A shadow of her former might.
A shadow that will fall all night.

A shadow.

YASMEEN *feeds the bow to the fire. It burns.*

ACKNOWLEDGEMENTS

I have been well supported in the writing of this play and have thanks
to give. Most notably to Ian Rickson, my friend and the director, who
brought the play to my attention, inviting me to get involved and make
my 'cover version'. Thank you, Ian, for your solidarity, your patience
and your expertise. Greek scholar Helen Eastman provided me with a
literal translation and hours of fascinating conversation about Greek
theatre: what it did, who it was for, how it worked, how it sounded.
Thank you, Helen. The first time I heard the original Sophocles play
read it was by a group of military veterans: Cassidy Little, Darren Swift,
Maurialla Simpson, Steve Shaw, Tobi Adeoke, Shaun Johnson, Andy
Macabre, Olaf Jones and Stewart Hill. Thank you all for the insights
you gave into how Sophocles' play resonated with you and your
experiences thousands of years later. It was inspiring and so useful for
me to have the chance to hear from and speak with you all. As the play
developed, I was lucky enough to workshop it many times. I would
like to thank the actors involved in those workshops for their input
and enthusiasm. So, thank you, Tia Bannon, Helen Belbin, Janet Kay,
Seroca Davis, Josie Walker, Rosie Hilal, Juma Sharkah, Zubin Varla,
Souad Faress, Evelyn Lockley, Carmen Monroe, Jaygann Ayeh, Rufus
Wright, Doreene Blackstock, Eve Steele, Sophie Melville, Doña Croll,
Clare Perkins, Danielle Vitalis, Emma Frankland, Jenet Le Lacheur,
Liadán Dunlea, Genesis Lynea, Sandy Mcdade, Thalissa Teixiera,
Jackie Clune, Jennifer Lim, Eva Magyar, Golda Rosheuvel, Mofetoluwa
Akande, and all the assistants, admin staff and stage managers that
helped run the sessions. Also, my thanks to Rufus Norris and all the
team at the National Theatre, for programming the play, supporting the
workshops, and believing in it enough to put it on in the Olivier, even
amongst all the chaos and calamity of COVID-19. My thanks to the cast
and crew of the production. I'm so grateful for what you have given, to
the music, the design, the props, the lighting, the text itself. I've been
stunned by the artistry of the many people involved in putting a show
like this on stage. Finally, deepest thanks to my love, Assia Ghendir,
who has been with me all the way from *Philoctetes* to *Paradise*: to all
the various islands that fed in to the creation of this island, to every
sharing of the text, through all the drafts, inspiring lines of dialogue.
Assia, you have been integral to the life force of this play. Thank you.